GCSE

English Coursework Techniques

a 15-week revision programme

Authors:

Roger Machin   **Peter Thomas**

Your questions answered

Q: What is the point of this book?

A: *The aims of this book are:*

- to provide **a clear understanding** of the skills you need to succeed in the coursework element of GCSE English
- to show **when** and **where** those skills need to be demonstrated
- to **practise** those skills and give you opportunities to **develop** them **on your own**
- to **explain** how **work is marked** by examiners
- to **provide** a **structured series of assignments** to meet coursework requirements

and, most important of all,

- to **enable you to gain those extra marks** which will improve your chance of **a higher grade**.

Q: But, surely, all I have to do is get my essays done on time to get a grade?

A: *Good coursework assignments can mean the difference between a C and a D, or E, an A* and a B ... and so on. There are many key areas that examiners look for that this book tells you about. Besides, it's not just writing. There's speaking and listening, too.*

Q: Speaking and listening? I'm good at the first one!

A: *Perhaps not as good as you think. There are lots of ways you can impress the 'examiner' (your teacher!) here too – and the mark is worth 20 per cent of your overall grade.*

Q: So, how is the book structured? How do I use it?

A: *Follow the 12 units in this book, which fit into the types of work you will be doing in class. Most of them can be done without your teacher's help – others can be 'dipped into' at particular times throughout the course. Each unit deals with a key part of coursework (for example – Unit 7, 'Discuss: Speaking and Listening'). Each unit is between six and 10 pages long and is split as follows:*

- *the opening section*   has a **sample source text** showing key features of the skill has **tasks** showing you how to apply them
- *the second section*   has another **sample text** showing **different** features has **new tasks** showing you how to **apply** these
- *the third section*   has a **coursework assignment** for you to do, with '**Making the Grade**' tips to help you
- *the final section*   has **examples** of **real students' work**, the **grades** they received and the **assessor's comments**.

Q: Does that mean my coursework is 'sorted'?

A: *You've still got to do the work – but this book will guide you towards that better grade. Good luck!*

Contents

Unit 1 Explain: *Speaking and Listening Coursework*

In this Unit you will read extracts from interviews in which people explain different things about themselves. In your Coursework Task, you will be interviewed about a chosen interest, ambition or issue.

Sample One The following interview was published in the magazine, *J17*. Amy, an 18-year-old with a 10-month-old baby, talks about her experiences and attitudes.

AMY'S STORY

Q Why did you get pregnant?

A I was on the Pill and used condoms, too, to protect myself against sexually transmitted diseases. But after going out with Martin – Sam's dad – for a while we stopped using condoms. I was ill and the doctor gave me antibiotics. Nobody explained that these could stop the Pill working until it was too late.

Q How did having a baby change your life?

A I had to grow up very quickly. I have no social life now. I'm 18 going on 30. I've got the responsibility of looking after Sam for at least 16 years and it's terrifying. Not that I don't love him, because I do.

Q Looking back now, would you have changed anything?

A When I realised I had a baby that I needed to look after I thought, 'What have I done?'. I wish I'd waited until we had a house and all the other things you're supposed to have for a baby. But I'd been with Martin for two years when I became pregnant, and we're still together. I love Sam and I wouldn't change that for anything.

Q Why do you believe there are so many teenage pregnancies in Britain?

A I think the main reason is that our sex education is rubbish. It's given far too late. I was about 14 when I had classes, and I knew a couple of girls who were already pregnant by then. It was all diagrams – this bit goes here and this happens. There was a mention of contraception but nothing about the emotional side of having sex or about relationships.

Q How would you change it?

A I'd introduce it in primary school – it's way too late by the time you're at secondary. I'd talk about the difficulties of being a teenage mum – it's very hard work. The emotional side has to be discussed, and contraception – various methods and where you can get them.

J17

Task 1

Key Features
We often explain experiences so that those who have not had them can understand what we know.

1. Read Amy's answers to the first **three** questions. She is explaining why she became pregnant and how the experience of having a baby has changed her life.

   Use information from the first three answers only.
   Write down **five** pieces of advice you think can be gained from Amy's experiences.

2. Why do you think Amy repeats herself at the end of answers 2 and 3?

Task 2

Key Features
We often need to explain opinions, especially if they are controversial.

1. Answer the following questions, based on Amy's explanations.

   ● What is the **difference** between a teenage pregnancy and an unwanted pregnancy?
   ● What does Amy think is **wrong** with sex education in Britain?
   ● How would she **improve** sex education?

2. Write a letter (of no more than 200 words) to *J17*.
   Explain your own views on Amy's experiences and opinions.

When you explain, you have a purpose – to show people why or how.

Sample Two

In this extract, Dave Hoover, an American lion tamer, is interviewed by *FHM* magazine.

Q How long does it take to train a wild cat?

A *Six months for lions, a little less for tigers – they're smarter. We start when they're 18 months old. I just sit inside the door of the cage with my cigar and a crossword until the animal is no longer worried by my being there. Next, we cut off the cat's food for a day, then start feeding him off the end of a stick. Then we put a seat in the cage; after a couple of days, I start feeding him while he's on there. That's my first command: "Seat." My act incorporates things the animals do naturally – they run, jump, lay down, roll over and sit up, so we have them jumping hurdles or walking backwards on a barrel.*

Q Do you have a favourite lion?

A *Yes. I had a big, black-maned lion called Caesar – a truly handsome cat, but who was meaner than the devil. He hospitalised me seven times, but he was more responsive than the other cats. Then one time in Philadelphia, a big lion charged me, my foot slipped and I went down. My stick caught the animal in the mouth and he was hanging over me. Caesar attacked the other lion and saved my life. He worked until he was 21; then, when I retired him to a safari park, he sired 32 cubs.*

Q Would a lion eat you if it had the chance?

A *No – they're not hungry enough. But a trainer I knew was killed in front of an audience after the door dropped on a big lion's tail and it jumped the guy. The cat carried my friend around like a rag doll. The police had to shoot the animal to get the body back.*

Q What's the closest you've been to death?

A *I was in hospital for three months not long after I started in the business. I needed 152 stitches in my legs and arms, and had to have a blood transfusion. A lion opened up the side of my leg – I have no feeling from my right knee down. It happened during training when, like a dummy, I'd gone along to the cage by myself. I was wearing a watch with an expanding wristband and when this lion swung at me, his claws got tangled in the band, and he pulled me into him. He was missing a fang or he* would have chewed off my finger and probably a toe. That scared the hell out of me. Fortunately, I always wear a steel collar for training – big cats often go for the throat – and I had heavy clothing on, although the lion ate my wool coat. They like mutton, apparently.*

Q Ever stuck your head in a lion's mouth?

A *No way! That trick was popular years ago: if the trainer felt pressure from the lion's jaws, he'd spit tobacco down its throat to make it open up. That's not to say some didn't lose their heads.*

Q What should we do if confronted with an escaped big cat?

A *Stay still or move away slowly. Nine times out of ten, the animal will move away from you. Don't run or he'll follow you – a lion can run 100 yards in four-and-a-half seconds.*

Task 3

1. Dave Hoover gives us lots of interesting information about himself and about lion taming in general.

   - Write down **10** facts we learn from the interview.
   - Next to each fact, write in brackets whether the information is about **Dave Hoover** or **lion taming in general**.

2. The original interview had more than 20 questions.

   - Write down at least **five more questions** you would like to ask Dave Hoover.
   - Try to ask questions that would provide you with **interesting information** about Dave Hoover and the business of lion taming.

FOCUS on detailed information

Task 4

1. Find **five time markers** used in Dave Hoover's first paragraph.

2. Write down a list of phrases in this interview that contain **numerical figures**. You should find at least 10.

3. Explain the effect of Dave Hoover's use of **time markers** and **numerical figures**.

TIME MARKER

long ago

next

later

Speaking and Listening Coursework Task

● This task works best in groups of between three and five people.

Each member of the group decides on a subject they can speak about in detail. Your subject could be either something personal to you from your own experience, or something you enjoy doing and know a lot about.

When you have decided on your subject, tell each other what it is. Each member of the group now thinks up at least five questions to ask for each of the subjects. When the questions are ready, each group member is given the chance to look at the ones they will be asked and to research the answers if necessary. When everyone agrees they have prepared enough, the interviews can take place.

REMEMBER
● you should explain facts, opinions and experiences
● your explanation should be as clear as possible (use time markers, or other organisational phrases).

Look at the following three questions:

1. When did you start playing football?
2. Why do you think so many people love football?
3. What was the most memorable football match you have ever played in?

These questions are designed to bring out either an experience, an opinion or a fact. Which is which? When you ask your own questions, try to produce a mixture of the three.

MAKING THE GRADE

To get a Grade 'C' you need not only to *gain* the listener's interest, but to *sustain* it, so you need to think of ways to keep re-interesting your listener at various points throughout the piece.

For a Grade 'A' you need to *involve* your listener, so you need to use some *rhetorical questions* or *refer* to what the listener may have thought or experienced in his/her own life.

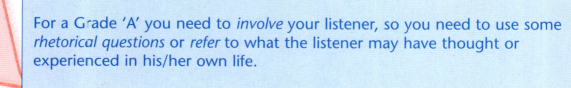

Other Students' Work

Here are extracts from two responses that show performance at different GCSE grades.

E

Q So when did you start running seriously?
A About three years ago.

Q What made you do it? What do you enjoy about it?
A I just like running. It makes me feel fit and I like it because I'm quite good.

Q Are you good? Have you won anything?
A Yes, I've won quite a lot, but nothing really big yet. I win most of the middle-distance races I take part in at school and I usually come first in the inter-school events. My times are good enough for county.

Q What are the benefits of being a runner?
A It makes you fit and it ... you waste less time watching TV.

Assessor's Comments

This candidate has not made the best use of the chances his interviewers have given him. There is very little he can do with the first question because it really only asks for a bare fact. With the second question, however, there is a real chance to go into detail about positive experiences of running. The same is true of the fourth question, which gives the speaker the opportunity to express his opinions on running and indeed exercise in general.

FOCUS

grade contrasts

B

Q Why have you chosen to talk about a car accident? Isn't it a bit morbid?
A Not really, because nothing terrible happened in it. I just got bad whiplash and nobody else was injured at all. It wasn't some great dramatic smash-up. The thing about it was, though, that it made me see a lot of things differently. For a split second, when the other car pulled in front of us, I thought I was going to die.

Q When did it happen?
A It was in Year 8, about three years ago, when I was coming back from school. I suppose ... I think that was actually another part of it. I was quite young and I never expected anything like that to happen. I was very secure and thinking about dinner and the weekend and then suddenly – bang! You realise you could be dead and everything would be totally finished ... your friends, school, your life, everything.

● **Explain** the **differences** between the second extract and the first.

Unit 2 Describe: *Speaking and Listening Coursework*

In this Unit you will read extracts from two descriptions. Your Coursework Task will be to describe how a new promotional video of your school could be filmed.

Sample One   The following description is from a directory of British schools. It describes Hunmanby Hall, a former girls' school in North Yorkshire.

HUNMANBY HALL SCHOOL

The Old Hall of the Mitford family estate provides the centre of the School which is set in 50 acres of parkland with magnificent woodlands to the south of the grounds, and views of Filey Bay.

The great majority of buildings are purpose-built and provide ample space for specialist teaching. Amongst the facilities are four well equipped science laboratories, two computer rooms, a new Music School, a Sports Hall, a purpose-built Sixth Form House, a modern self-service layout in the Dining Hall, and a Theatre Arts Room.

The policy of the School is to maintain the buildings to the highest standard and constantly to improve, develop and modernise the facilities to meet the changing needs of education.

One of the great strengths of Hunmanby Hall is its size. We are small enough to be able to live out in practice one of the foundation principles of the School – that the individual matters: yet we are large enough to be able to offer the essential breadth of opportunity in both academic and creative subjects which will enable each girl to develop her special abilities and which will help to equip her in every way for the demands and opportunities of the twenty-first century in which she will spend the greater part of her adult life.

We are proud of our high academic standards but we are equally proud of our ability to draw out and encourage the latent talents of the pupil who is less able academically. Preparation is given up to university scholarship standard in both the Arts and Sciences, while for the less academic Sixth Formers there is a one-year vocational course.

A number of scholarships for entry at 11 and 14 are available. A generous number of Sixth Form scholarships are also awarded on the basis of an interview and school report. Please contact the Secretary for details of these and for a prospectus and video cassette.

Task 1

Key Features
Good descriptions usually contain lots of detail.

1. Write a list of **10** items of **factual** information provided in the description of Hunmanby Hall. Try as far as possible to use your own words. Include only **one** fact under **each bullet**. You could start:

- The centre of the school is provided by the old hall of the Mitford estate.

- It is set in 50 acres of parkland.

2. Read the passage again. Write down **five** questions you would ask the Headteacher to find out **extra information** about the school.

Task 2

Key Features
Informative descriptions can also be used to persuade.

Sometimes descriptions are a subtle mix of fact *and* opinion.

1. The description of Hunmanby Hall is designed to attract people, especially parents, to the school. Make a list of six phrases that are intended to make the school appear at its best.

For example:

Hunmanby Hall has 'magnificent woodlands'.
('magnificent' = an opinion, 'woodlands' = a fact about the school)

2. Imagine that one of the girls currently attending Hunmanby Hall has been asked to write a section of the prospectus. Write a paragraph from her point of view. Include descriptions that you think will persuade other students to come to the school.

- Use the information already provided, but make up other details if you need to.

Sample Two

This extract describes the experiences of a boy on his first day at a new school.

I'd never seen Cronton School until the morning I started there. My mother took me in the car, dropping me at the gate.

She grinned at me and said, "Now it's up to you."

I walked straight in, looking forward in an odd, excited way to being the same as other kids. The school was just as my mother had described it, a grouping of shoe-box shapes made of concrete and glass, with the brilliant green of an overgrown playing-field stretching away behind it towards the distance where the hills were.

I walked along the front of the school and round a corner and I was in the playground. In front of me were hundreds of boys doing the things I had never done. They were wrestling and rolling and screaming and shouting. They were darting and dashing so swiftly that the patterns of their movements made me dizzy, while their noise deafened me.

In a corner of the playground I met loneliness for the first time in my life. Loneliness isn't being alone but wondering why you have to be alone. I had rarely known other kids, I had always been alone, yet in those first moments at school I felt loneliness flood through me as I watched the hundreds of boys. My brain ached as their uproar beat against it. They and I were all wearing the same uniform, but they were different from me. They were rough savages, screaming their war-cries and rushing into brutal battle, and they were happy in a way I had never known. They were happy shouting at each other, wrestling each other, hating each other.

Then one of them spotted me and, like a dog catching a strange scent, he swerved and stopped in front of me. He was smaller than I was and his thick glasses gave him the look of an owl.

"You a new kid?" he asked.

I nodded.

"What's your name?"

"Stewart," I said. He was shooting his questions at me like bullets and I didn't like them.

"Stewart what?" he asked.

"Jimmy Stewart."

"Jimmy Stewart," he said as if tasting the name. Then he went into a convulsive dance and started screaming, "*Jimmy Stewpot! Jimmy Stewpot!*"

I was so astonished that I just stared at him and didn't at first see the other boys his voice had attracted. They came gathering round and while he went on jerking like a Dervish they studied me. He was red-faced and hoarse, his spectacles were on the end of his nose, he was a nightmare of a boy yet they watched me.

"He's a new kid!" he yelled. "His name's Jimmy Stewpot!"

I could see dozens of pairs of eyes and I knew how zoo animals must feel on Sunday afternoons when people press close to the cages. There was a dull kind of interest in all the eyes; interest and animosity, but no friendliness. I felt lonelier than ever.

From 'The Dragon in the Garden' by Reginald Maddock

Task 3

Key Features
Descriptions should give a clear impression of people and things.

1. In your own words write down your immediate impressions of

- Jimmy's mum

- the school

- the boys in the playground

- the boy whose glasses make him look like an owl.

FOCUS
clear description

2. Now write part of an advertisement for Cronton School. You need to adopt a consistent style for the audience and the purpose. The audience is parents keen to choose the best for their children, and your purpose is to impress them that the school will be caring and professional, so your language should not slip into casual, informal or humorous uses. Your section of the advertisement must include information about:

- the school buildings
- the behaviour of the boys
- the way that students new to the school are treated.

Task 4

Key Features
The person describing a scene may include attitudes and opinions which influence the reader's view of it.

1. Make a list of **six** of the **thoughts** or **feelings** expressed by Jimmy on his first day at Cronton School.

2. The description on page 12 is written from Jimmy's point of view. Rewrite the morning's events as they might be described by

- the Headteacher
- Jimmy's mother
- the boy who looks like an owl.

Speaking and Listening Coursework Task

scenes

Your school is about to produce a new promotional video. The idea is to present the school in the best possible way.

Your task is to decide what the opening scenes of the video should be, then describe the opening scenes to an audience. Your audience will ask you questions about your material, so be prepared to explain your decisions.

- The video as a whole will be between 12 and 15 minutes long.
- You should aim to design at least the first 10 scenes.

Promotional videos normally have 'voiceovers'. Do not try to write a voiceover yourself, just explain the *kind* of thing that would be said, with a few quotations. Use the example below to help you.

Scene Four

A shot of the Science labs, probably room 42, as this is the best equipped. Voiceover will talk about how this is 'the most recently modernised laboratory in the county' and goes on to say how essential the equipment and material is for modern science investigation, particularly at GCSE and A level. Students should be in the room conducting some kind of experiment. We'll need to make sure they're wearing goggles to suggest practical work carried out in safe conditions ...

REMEMBER
- give a clear and detailed description of those aspects of the school you are presenting on the video
- do not forget that your description is meant to present the school in a positive way
- you should also be prepared to explain the decisions you have made.

MAKING THE GRADE

To get a Grade 'C' you will need to *show a consistent style of delivery*. In other words, you must speak descriptively throughout your presentation. Choose vocabulary that suits your purpose and your intended audience.

To get a Grade 'A' you will need to *show cogency* (persuasive force) and *explicit depth of detail*. You must be absolutely clear at all times so that the listener knows exactly what is going to take place in your video. You also need to explain why you have made particular decisions. In the extract above, for instance, the speaker has explained why she thinks room 42 should be used in preference to others.

Other Students' Work

Here are extracts from two responses that show performance at different GCSE grades.

D

Interviewer	**So how are you going to start your video?**
Luke	I'm going to start with a picture of Mrs Berg (the Headteacher). She's going to be talking into the camera ...
Interviewer	**And she's going to be speaking?**
Luke	Yes. She'll be saying, like, ... "Welcome to North Green School. Over the next 15 minutes we want to show you just how much we have to offer."
Interviewer	**She'll be in the office?**
Luke	No ... She's going to be standing out at the front of the school round by the grass and the trees. You know where the board is that says 'North Green' on it? So, she's standing there and the idea is that she's in the middle of all this, not countryside, but like a park. And when she speaks you can see the name of the school above her shoulder.

FOCUS *grade contrasts*

B

Interviewer	**And your sixth scene is in the music room ... is that right?**
Luke	It's in the music room and the camera's over by the store cupboard so that you get a picture, like, of outside as well – you know where the music room looks out over the trees? So if you're watching it you think, 'Oh, right, so the school's in a really nice place and the teachers and the kids who go there must be nice as well.' And then these kids play their music and the voiceover says, "We consider music to be a very important part of education at North Green." The students, they're probably Year 7 or 8, are all smiling and you get a picture of Mr Carney (the music teacher) conducting them to show that this is a really professional lesson that's going on ...

Explain
- **why** Luke's second description is **better** than his first
- **how** his second description could have been **improved** even further.

Unit 3   Narrate: *Speaking and Listening Coursework*

 In this Unit   you will read two narrative extracts. In your Coursework Task, you will narrate a personal experience of your own.

Sample One

In the extract below, a survivor from the *Titanic* describes his fight for survival after being washed overboard.

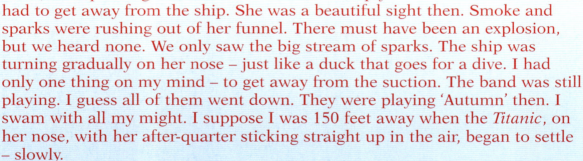

The big wave carried the boat off. I had hold of an oarlock and I went with it. The next I knew I was in the boat. But that was not all. I was in the boat, and the boat was upside down, and I was under it. And I remember realising I was wet through and that whatever happened I must not breathe, for I was under water. I knew I had to fight for it, and I did. How I got out from under the boat I do not know but I felt a breath of air at last. There were men all round me – hundreds of them. The sea was dotted with them, all depending on their lifebelts. I felt I simply had to get away from the ship. She was a beautiful sight then. Smoke and sparks were rushing out of her funnel. There must have been an explosion, but we heard none. We only saw the big stream of sparks. The ship was turning gradually on her nose – just like a duck that goes for a dive. I had only one thing on my mind – to get away from the suction. The band was still playing. I guess all of them went down. They were playing 'Autumn' then. I swam with all my might. I suppose I was 150 feet away when the *Titanic*, on her nose, with her after-quarter sticking straight up in the air, began to settle – slowly.

When at last the waves washed over her rudder there wasn't the least bit of suction I could feel. She must have kept going just so slowly as she had been... I felt after a little while like sinking. I was very cold. I saw a boat of some kind near me, and put all of my strength into an effort to swim to it. It was hard work. I was all done when a hand reached out from the boat and pulled me aboard. It was our same collapsible. The same crowd was on it. There was just room for me to roll on the edge. I lay there not caring what happened. Somebody sat on my legs. They were wedged in between slats and were being wrenched. I had not the heart left to ask the man to move. It was a terrible sight all around – men swimming and sinking.

Harold Bride

Task 1

Key Features
Narrative is often structured to sequence events in time.

1. Make a list of things that happen to Harold Bride. You could begin:

   ● carried overboard with the boat
   ● finds himself in the water 'under' the boat.

2. 'Time markers' are words and phrases that help the reader by giving a clear indication of when things happen. Harold Bride uses three.

TIME MARKER

The **next** I knew

When **at last**

After a **little while**

   Make a list of five other time markers and agree with a partner appropriate places they could fit in the narrative.

Task 2

Key Features
Narratives can be made more interesting if they do more than present events in time sequence – they can include personal thoughts and feelings, for example.

1. Read the following sentence:

   ● And I remember realising I was wet through and that whatever happened I must not breathe.

   Write down **five** other sentences that show Harold Bride's **personal thoughts** and **feelings**.

2. Now add a paragraph to Harold Bride's narrative. Imagine him as an old man looking back at the day the *Titanic* sank.

Sample Two

In his book *Fever Pitch,* Nick Hornby writes about his life as an Arsenal supporter. In the following extract he narrates an experience he had in his early days as a teacher.

On my second or third day, I asked a group of third years to write down on a piece of paper their favourite book, favourite song, favourite film and so on, and went around the class talking to them all in turn. This was how I discovered that the bad boy at the back, the one with the mod haircut and the permanent sneer (and the one, inevitably, with the biggest vocabulary and the best writing style), was completely consumed by all things Arsenal, and I pounced. But when I had made my confession, there was no meeting of minds, or fond, slow-motion embrace; instead, I received a look of utter contempt. "You?" he said. "You? What do *you* know about it?"

For a moment I saw myself through his eyes, a pillock in a tie with an ingratiating smile, desperately trying to worm my way into places I had no right to be, and understood. But then something else – a rage born out of thirteen years of Highbury hell, probably, and an unwillingness to abandon one of the most important elements of my self-identity to chalky, tweedy facelessness – took over, and I went mad.

The madness took a strange form. I wanted to grab that kid by the lapels and bang him against the wall, and yell at him, over and over again, "I know more than you ever will, you snotty little f***wit!" but I knew that this was not advisable. So I spluttered for a few seconds, and then to my surprise (I watched them as they spewed forth) a torrent of quiz questions gushed out of me. "Who scored for us in the '69 League Cup Final? Who went in goal when Bob Wilson got carried off in '72 at Villa Park? Who did we get from Spurs, in exchange for David Jenkins? Who ...?" On and on I went; the boy sat there, the questions bouncing off the top of his head like snowballs, while the rest of the class watched in bemused silence.

Task 3

1. Make a list of **six** phrases or sentences that Nick Hornby uses to create **humour**. Next to each of them, briefly **explain how** the humour has been used. You could start with:

| I pounced | *makes him seem like some sort of wild animal* |

2. **Read** the second and third paragraphs again. **Rewrite** them in a **serious** style. You could begin:

> For a moment I saw myself through his eyes, a *pillock* in a tie *with an ingratiating smile*.
>
> For a moment I saw myself through his eyes, a *foolish teacher wearing a tie*, *smiling in an ingratiating way*.

3. Explain the effect that changing the style has had.

Task 4

1. We learn a lot about Nick Hornby in this extract. List **six** phrases that tell us something about him, **explaining** for each of them what we have learned. You could begin:

| favourite book, favourite song, favourite film | *He seems like someone who wants to get to know his students.* |

2. Write a paragraph of your own describing something that has happened to you. You could write about a time when you:

- tried to persuade someone to do something they didn't want to
- were unfairly punished for something
- did something you know you shouldn't have
- had a serious disagreement with someone else.

Make your narrative as detailed as possible. When you have finished, write a brief summary of what you think the narrative reveals about your personality.

Speaking and Listening Coursework Task

Prepare a talk in which you narrate an experience you have had. You could talk about:

- the experience you described in Task 4
- something funny that has happened to you
- an experience that had a dramatic effect on you.

REMEMBER
- pay attention to the **time** order
- bring out your own **thoughts** and **feelings**
- use **humour** if appropriate
- speak in **detail**.

MAKING THE GRADE

To get a Grade 'C' you will need to *sustain the interest of the listener**. This means that your talk should use at least some of the key features you have encountered in this unit. Even if the content is not dramatic, the use of these features will keep your listeners interested.

To get a Grade 'A' you must *show cogency**, which is the power to make people want to agree with you. This can be done by appealing to reason, by giving a personal anecdote, by referring to an expert or by humorously exaggerating an opposite view. Being cogent means being compelling – making readers feel that they can accept what you say.

* The words in italics (which you will see throughout the book) come directly from the exam board Mark Scheme.

Other Students' Work

Here is a transcript of part of a narration by Nancie, a Year 10 student. Her talk was awarded a Grade 'A'.

Nancie has made frequent use of the key features of narrative. Examples of where she has done so are in bold and have been numbered so you can find them more easily. (The key feature about detail has been left out because it is a general one. It refers to the whole of the talk so it cannot be identified in a phrase or sentence.) When you have finished reading, write down the number of each bolded phrase and identify which key feature is demonstrated. Using them in your own talk will help raise your grade.

A

I was about eight years old **at the time (1)** and my dad had promised me we could go ice skating. One **Saturday afternoon (2)**, we picked up two of my friends, Kathy and Sadiya, from their houses. We piled into the car and drove to the rink. It **seemed like a massive place (3)** to me and there was a kind of echo, a background hum of people's voices, and laughing and screaming. I had no idea what was going on but I remember **feeling really excited (4)**. It was something totally different from anything I'd done before. It seems silly now to have got so excited about something as little as going ice skating, but that was the way I felt. Kathy and Sadiya felt the same way as well, because we were all giggling and joking about what we were going to do.

My dad took us up to the counter where you hire the skates. I told the lady there what my shoe size was and she handed over a pair of skates that **felt really heavy to me (5)**. We walked over to the rink and put them on. Then we lumbered on to the ice. Everyone else was skating round incredibly quickly but we could hardly stand up. Kathy slipped over and pulled Sadiya down and Sadiya pulled me down with her. This went on for **about five minutes (6)** without us getting any distance from where we had started. My dad was in skates as well but he just looked at us laughing while he held on to the side. Eventually we realised that we'd never do anything if we just held on to each other. So we all grabbed hold of the wall on the side of the rink and started moving slowly around.

I could see Kathy and Sadiya on the other side of the rink trying desperately to stand on their feet. **I realised I must look as odd as they did (7)**. Nobody paid us any attention, though, and I gradually **felt confident (8)** enough to let go of the side. The amazing thing is that when you do get the confidence it comes very quickly and you feel as if you can start moving around really fast. That's what I did. **For a few minutes (9)**, I had a real rush of freedom as I moved around at the same pace as everyone else. When I slipped over **I felt like a complete idiot (10)**, but if you stick with it, it does become much easier.

All the while my dad was going through the same experience as we were. He'd been laughing at all of us but when he got away from the side he was just as bad as we were. He got confident faster than we did, though, and he really paid for it. He was out in the middle of the rink and I saw his legs go from under him. From instinct, he grabbed out with his hands and **pulled a teenage girl on top of him (11)**. She looked at him in a **totally disgusted way (12)** and then skated off without looking back.

Unit 4 Explore: *Wide Reading Coursework*

In this Unit you will read passages from writing that explores the relationships between different texts. Your first Coursework Task will be to compare at least two of the texts you have read in class. In your second Coursework Task you will discuss possible links between texts.

Sample One In this extract, Ashley Sheldon writes about two fictional murderers: Grimesby Roylott, from Sir Arthur Conan Doyle's 'The Speckled Band', and Mary Maloney, from Roald Dahl's 'Lamb to the Slaughter'.

It would certainly seem that Grimesby Roylott is the less forgivable of the two murderers. The murder of Julia Stoner is committed for purely financial benefit. He knows that if his stepdaughter marries, as she has told him she is about to, he will lose a lot of money and for that reason alone he decides she must die. Julia's murder is carefully planned and the investigating police find no evidence that her death is in any way suspicious. When Helen Stoner, Julia's sister, announces her engagement two years after the murder, Dr Roylott's reaction is exactly the same. He moves Helen into Julia's room and sends the deadly pit viper up through the ventilation outlet while she is sleeping. It is good fortune on the part of Helen Stoner that she gets Sherlock Holmes on to the case in time. Dr Roylott appears to have no worries about sending two young women to their deaths in the most painful way, simply because their continued existence is financially inconvenient to him. By contrast, Mary Maloney murders her husband during a fit of passion. She kills him because he tells her he is leaving her. To make things worse, she is 'six months pregnant' and believes she and her husband have the perfect relationship. He misunderstands her emotions so badly that he tells her she need not worry about money and should not make a 'fuss' because it 'wouldn't be very good' for his job. She goes, in a daze, to get his dinner (a leg of lamb) and before she knows what she is doing smashes it down on the back of his head and kills him. To properly understand her actions, we need to go back to the 1950s when divorce and separation were less common and more shameful than nowadays. Mary Maloney would see her broken marriage as a statement that she had failed as a woman. This is part of the reason that she reacts so emotionally.

It is possible, perhaps, to see Grimesby Roylott's crimes in a different light. Dr Roylott has in some respects been a victim of circumstances. His family wasted a large fortune and left him with no money to look after a manor house. He tried his best to establish a medical practice in India but this failed after he was the target of a number of burglaries. The murder of Julia Stoner and the attempted murder of her sister were not intended to make him rich: they were simply to leave him with enough to get by on. His motive, then, was not greed, but fear of poverty. In the Victorian period, a fall from wealth and position was considered a shameful thing, and rich people would often do anything to avoid it.

Task 1

Key Features
Exploration should consider alternative interpretations and responses.

1. Read these two sentences:

a. Grimesby Roylott is evil.

b. Grimesby Roylott is a victim.

From your reading of Ashley Sheldon's analysis, note down the **evidence** that supports these two statements.

2. Find a recent newspaper report that criticises an individual or a group of people for behaving in an unacceptable way. Write a paragraph interpreting their actions in a less negative light.

   ● You could refer to the behaviour of the characters and the language of the author. The aim is not to pretend that the behaviour did not happen but to **explain** it so that it does not seem so bad.

3. Pick one of the characters from a novel or short story you have read recently. Choose one of their important actions. Write a paragraph considering as many possible reasons for their actions as you can.

Task 2

Key Features
It is important to show how texts reflect the cultural contexts in which they were written. This involves attitudes, beliefs or customs common at the time of writing.

1. In your own words, explain how cultural context (that is, time and society) is used to explain elements of the behaviour of Grimesby Roylott and Mary Maloney.

2. Read a short story that was written before 1914.

   ● Write a list of things in the story that seem **strange** or **out of place** to you as a twenty-first century reader.
   ● Compare your list with a partner and add other findings to your list.
   ● Write a paragraph **explaining** how the behaviour of the characters is affected by the **cultural context**. This may involve comment on social class, gender, or attitudes and beliefs.

Sample Two   The following extract is taken from an essay in which Jenny Ngeti explores the portrayal of women in 'The Son's Veto' by Thomas Hardy, 'The Yellow Wallpaper' by Charlotte Perkins Gilman and 'Survival' by John Wyndham. This passage concentrates on 'The Yellow Wallpaper' and 'Survival'.

The Narrator of 'The Yellow Wallpaper' is looked down upon by all the other characters in the story, most notably her husband. He calls her his 'little goose', an expression he believes to be affectionate, but one that also shows he thinks of her as a child. He thinks he is helping her but of course he is not. He sees her as a mentally weak person who needs to be kept in her room away from all excitement and contact with other people, when actually that is exactly what she needs. The longer she is kept in isolation the more depressed she becomes. Her depression stems from boredom and when she is bored she imagines things in the wallpaper. At first she only sees shapes and patterns. Then she imagines the paper is alive and that people (other women like herself) are trapped behind it or being strangled in its web. Eventually she becomes completely insane and tears the wallpaper off the wall, hoping to release the prisoners inside. The hope that exists for her at the beginning of the story has completely disappeared by the end.

In 'Survival', Alice Morgan is also seen as feeble-minded by the other characters. Her mother says that she is like a 'little mouse' and the captain of the spaceship calls her a 'poor little thing'. Like the Narrator of 'The Yellow Wallpaper', Alice Morgan is thought of as a person who needs protection from a cruel world. The reason for this in both cases is that the people involved are women. In 'The Yellow Wallpaper' the protection is suffocating and causes the Narrator's madness. In 'Survival', the protection is unnecessary. Alice Morgan shows in many ways that she is stronger than the men on board the spaceship. When the ship is drifting out of control and the remaining passengers have a lottery to decide who will be slaughtered to provide food for the others, Alice refuses, saying that she is carrying a baby. When the men try to bully her, she tells them that if they kill her they will be tried for murder even if they do survive. In a way, Alice Morgan's strength causes her madness, just as the Narrator's desire for freedom in 'The Yellow Wallpaper' leads to another type of insanity. When she is left alone on the ship and help finally arrives, her instinct for survival leads her to shoot (and presumably eat) her potential rescuers.

The way in which both stories are written is interesting. 'The Yellow Wallpaper' is written in extremely short sentences and paragraphs, almost as if the Narrator is too distracted to maintain a particular thought for any length of time. The vocabulary is quite complex and this suggests an educated woman able to express herself in an intelligent way. 'Survival', on the other hand, is written in a very direct, simple style in which people say things like "Get on with it, man". The language implies that this is a hard, straight-talking, 'man's world'. This only serves to emphasise the fact that Alice Morgan is an extremely tough woman.

Task 3

1. Write down two similarities and one difference between the Narrator of 'The Yellow Wallpaper' and Alice Morgan from 'Survival'.

2. Both women change during the stories described by Jenny Ngeti. **Write a paragraph describing the way a character familiar to you has** changed. You could write about:

   - a person you know
   - a character in a book or a film.

FOCUS

comparing

Task 4

1. Read again the last paragraph of Jenny Ngeti's account. Here she writes about not *what* the writers have said about the characters but *how* they have said it.

   What three conclusions about the women does Jenny Ngeti come to in this paragraph?

2. Read a couple of paragraphs from a novel or short story. Explain *how* the story is being told and *why* the writer is choosing to tell it in this way.

   You could focus on reasons for:

   - the **length** or **complexity** of the sentences
   - the **vocabulary** used (is it simple or complex? does it use slang or informal language?)
   - use of strong **images**, use of **metaphor**
   - specific language **structures** (such as noun phrases, powerful verbs and so on)
   - any use of **humour**.

Wide Reading Coursework Task

Compare and **contrast** at least **two works of fiction**. You will need to choose a **common aspect** of the two texts such as 'childhood' or 'the portrayal of relationships'.

- One of the short stories or novels must have been written by a named author **before 1914**.

- The other must have been written **after 1914**.

- Your teacher will help you decide on the works of fiction to study, what aspect to focus on, and the types of comparisons you need to make between the texts.

Dos and Don'ts

REMEMBER
- consider alternative interpretations of actions and attitude, and different responses to them
- the influence of cultural contexts on attitudes, behaviour and ideas is important
- make comparisons (including contrasts) *between* texts – show how things stay the same or change *within* texts
- write about the way the story has been told and give possible reasons why
- make your comparisons as you are going along. Do not write everything you can think of about one of the texts – and then everything you can think of about the other.

MAKING THE GRADE

To get a Grade 'C' you will need to *show insight when discussing style, structure and characters.* This means that you must understand how the writers' *characteristic* choice of language makes their fiction more interesting.

To get a Grade 'A' you will need to recognise *writers' inventiveness with language.* You will have to show that you understand how decisions made by the writer about his or her specific choices of language can have a significant impact on how their fiction is read. You must also write about the behaviour of characters as thoughtfully as you can for *emotive, ironic or figurative effect.*

Other Students' Work

The following extracts are from assignments by the same student, Ashraf. In Year 10, he wrote a comparison of the settings in two short stories, 'A Terribly Strange Bed' by Wilkie Collins, and 'Farthing House' by Susan Hill. His work was given a Grade 'C'. After discussing his assignment with an English teacher, he decided to redraft it in Year 11 and was awarded an 'A'.

C Mrs Flower's first impression of Farthing House is a very good one. Although it smells a bit of antiseptic, there is also a nicer smell of furniture polish and baking bread. She likes the antiques in the hall and also the cat that sleeps by the fire. It makes the atmosphere nice and homely. Her Aunt Addy is staying at Farthing House and her room is nice as well. She has all her own old furniture in it. Mrs Flower is staying in Cedar Room. It is big and has red curtains in it and it looks out over a garden. The Narrator of 'A Terribly Strange Bed' does not really like the place where he goes gambling. He says that the atmosphere in the room is like a tragedy and there is a man looking at him with vulture's eyes. After he goes to bed, he looks around the room he is sleeping in and he does not like it at all. He thinks the room is dirty and the chest of drawers is broken. He thinks the picture hanging on the wall is horrible because the man in it is weird and he looks as if he is going to be hanged.

FOCUS

grade contrast

A Mrs Flower's first impressions of Farthing House are mixed. She likes the smell of the furniture polish, the chrysanthemums and the baking bread and she thinks the cat by the fire is homely. In the background, though, is the 'smell of hospital antiseptic' which depresses her and she 'feels' a sense of 'something sinister' that she cannot describe. Her Aunt Addy's room is comfortable and the Cedar Room that she is staying in herself appears to be perfectly fine. But when Aunt Addy tells her that the room has only just become vacant, Mrs Flower gets another of those feelings that passes over her 'like a shadow'. The overall feeling created in this section of the story is that things are all right on the surface but that underneath there is a problem. The tension is being built up for when Mrs Flower sees the ghost later on in the story.

The opening of 'A Terribly Strange Bed' is told in a very different way. Wilkie Collins puts all his cards on the table immediately and the reader is never under the impression that the gambling house is anything more than a sleazy dump. There is a sense all around of 'mute, weird tragedy' and the characters he comes across are vile, like the wrinkled old man 'with the vulture eyes'. In 'Farthing House', the uneasiness is beneath the surface but in 'A Terribly Strange Bed' it is obvious from the start that things are not right. It is as if Wilkie Collins is making the reader ask how much worse it can get. When the Narrator goes to his bed, this question starts to be answered. The room is filthy and horribly furnished. The worst feature is the picture of the man who looks about to be hanged. It is almost as if this is the fate that might await the Narrator – this is obviously included by the writer to build up the tension.

Identify places in the 'A' grade extract where:

- Ashraf discusses **alternative interpretations** of 'Farthing House'
- he makes comparisons **within** and **between** the two texts
- he considers Wilkie Collins' narrative craft.

Sample Three

This is the beginning of a conversation between Damian Connolly and Janet Olsen which explores the possibility of an assignment comparing *Silas Marner* by George Eliot and *Animal Farm* by George Orwell.

JO   I mean – do you think there really are any serious links between these two texts?

DC   I think there are. Both stories have a real element of corruption in them. The wealthy and the powerful misuse their positions and there's nothing anyone can do about it.

JO   Go on.

DC   Well, think about Squire Cass and his family. All they do is drink and eat and they get gout and apoplexy because they're so greedy. The poor people in Raveloe don't complain about it either because they're scared to or it doesn't occur to them. The same thing happens in *Animal Farm*. Jones mistreats all the animals because they don't matter to him and he spends most of his time drunk. When Napoleon and the other pigs get control of the farm they do exactly the same thing.

JO   So power corrupts people – is that the idea?

DC   Yes – and it makes liars of them as well. Godfrey Cass is a pathetic liar. Squealer spends most of his time lying to the other animals.

JO   What other links can you see?

DC   There's the thing about closed community. You know where people are thrown out of a social group because they don't fit? Silas Marner is thrown out of Lantern Yard because he was supposed to have stolen the money and Snowball gets thrown off Animal Farm because Napoleon doesn't like him.

JO   Yes. But that is a bit different, Damian. The people in Lantern Yard really believe Silas stole the money. Snowball's thrown out of Animal Farm because he's a political threat to Napoleon.

DC   OK. I'm not saying they're necessarily identical, though. If you were doing an assignment on this you could make the point that the reasons for Silas and Snowball being thrown out of a closed community were different.

JO   I do agree with that. But do you really think that there are enough links between the two texts? They seem very different to me. I mean, *Silas Marner* is about a lonely miser who finds love. *Animal Farm* is about how good ideas often don't work out in practice. Surely there isn't that much of a relationship between them?

Task 5

Key Features
The links made between texts should be significant ones.

1. Wide reading assignments sometimes don't work because the links between the texts are simply not important. For example, it is true but not particularly interesting to say that Squire Cass in *Silas Marner* and Mr Jones in *Animal Farm* are both men.

2. Write down a list of at least five important similarities between two of the texts you have read during your GCSE course.

3. Compare your list with a partner's. Add any new links to your own list.

Write a list of four **significant** links between *Silas Marner* and *Animal Farm* as identified by Damian.

Task 6

Key Features
Exploratory conversations should prompt others to develop what they say, and should build on what they have said.

1. Explain why this is a key feature.

2. Make a list of five phrases Janet Olsen uses to be encouraging.

3. Read the following five phrases. For each of them, write out a less aggressive way of saying the same thing.

- *You're wrong.*

- *I disagree with you.*

- *There's no way these two texts can be compared with each other.*

- *What are you talking about?*

- *That is a link between the two texts but it's not one worth talking about.*

Keep your list to refer to later.

Wide Reading Coursework Task

Choose two works of fiction you have read on your GCSE course. With a partner, discuss the possible links and relationships between the texts.

- One of the texts should have been written **before 1914**.

- The other text should have been written **after 1914**.

- Your texts do not have to be closely linked. Your task is to explore whether there really are worthwhile and interesting comparisons to be made.

REMEMBER
- you should explore whether the links are significant
- your discussion should be supportive.

MAKING THE GRADE

To get a Grade 'C' you must *show insight when discussing similarities and differences in implications and relevance of texts.* This means you should explore how closely related your two texts are. It will be important to identify which of the links are important.

To get a Grade 'A' you will need to *make apt and careful comparison* between *moral* and *philosophical aspects* of texts. You must explain why different feelings, ideas and attitudes are valued by a writer, and why others are presented as dangers or weaknesses.

Other Students' Work

Two Year 11 students, Rahul and Blake, were asked to explore the possible relationships between Charlotte Brontë's *Jane Eyre* and Barry Hines' *A Kestrel for a Knave*. Both were awarded a Grade 'F' for their work. The extract below is taken from the beginning of their conversation.

> **F**
>
> **Rahul**   The relationship is childhood.
>
> **Blake**   The way that, like, Jane Eyre's childhood is really bad and so is Billy Casper's.
>
> **Rahul**   Jane has no friends and she's really poor. She lives all that way from her family and nobody cares about her at all. Billy is poor too.
>
> **Blake**   And Billy hasn't got any friends except for his hawk.
>
> **Rahul**   The teachers bully him too. Like the sports teacher makes him go in the shower.
>
> **Blake**   Jane Eyre's teachers bully her. Except Miss Temple. And in *Kes*, Mr Farthing is really nice to Billy.

Before you read the Assessor's comments, answer the questions below.

- Have Rahul and Blake discussed whether the comparisons are **significant**?
- Have they used words and phrases that are **encouraging** each other?

Now read the Assessor's Comments:

Assessor's Comments

Rahul and Blake have both made comparisons between the texts and have been given credit for this. They show that they understand that links can be made. However, they do not in any way explore possible relationships. Rahul's opening comment shows that he has already made up his mind about what the main link is to be. Throughout the conversation, neither Rahul nor Blake breaks away from what they have already decided to talk about. They do not encourage each other to branch out and follow new lines of thought: notice that they don't ask each other any questions about the relationship between the two novels. Blake, for example, could have asked Rahul in what ways Jane Eyre was poor and whether her poverty was similar to or different from Billy Casper's. This is what is meant by exploring an issue, and neither Rahul nor Blake has done this in any depth. They have stated some facts but not considered causes, effects or writers' purposes. Nor have they given their own responses to what they have read.

Unit 5 Analyse: *Shakespeare and Twentieth-Century Drama Coursework*

In this Unit you will read extracts from three analyses. Two of them are of Shakespeare plays and one is of *An Inspector Calls* by J B Priestley. In your first Coursework Task you will be writing about a scene from a Shakespeare play. In your second task, you will be interviewed as one of the actors in a production of a modern drama text.

Sample One

In the following sample, Mario Goodwin analyses his own performance as Sir Andrew Aguecheek in the 'box tree' scene from *Twelfth Night*. Sir Andrew is a foolish character and Mario is writing about how he tried to communicate that foolishness to the audience.

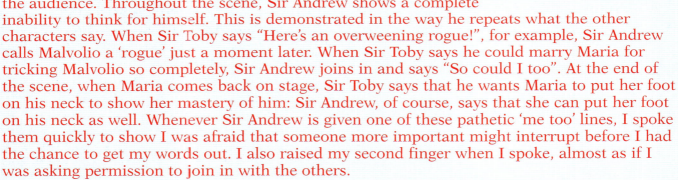

This is the scene in which Sir Toby, Fabian and Sir Andrew hide behind the box tree to watch Malvolio making a fool of himself. Malvolio is strutting around imagining he is more than just a steward and that the beautiful Lady Olivia has a crush on him. When he finds the forged letter that Sir Toby's 'close friend', Maria, has dropped in his way, he becomes totally convinced that Olivia adores him.

This is a comic scene not only because Malvolio is being shown up as so conceited. Sir Andrew, too, is made to look a fool by his silly comments and asides. It was my job to communicate his silliness to the audience. Throughout the scene, Sir Andrew shows a complete inability to think for himself. This is demonstrated in the way he repeats what the other characters say. When Sir Toby says "Here's an overweening rogue!", for example, Sir Andrew calls Malvolio a 'rogue' just a moment later. When Sir Toby says he could marry Maria for tricking Malvolio so completely, Sir Andrew joins in and says "So could I too". At the end of the scene, when Maria comes back on stage, Sir Toby says that he wants Maria to put her foot on his neck to show her mastery of him: Sir Andrew, of course, says that she can put her foot on his neck as well. Whenever Sir Andrew is given one of these pathetic 'me too' lines, I spoke them quickly to show I was afraid that someone more important might interrupt before I had the chance to get my words out. I also raised my second finger when I spoke, almost as if I was asking permission to join in with the others.

Probably the worst moment for Sir Andrew, not that he realises it, comes when Malvolio is imagining himself in the fantasy role of Olivia's husband. With his new-found power, Malvolio, thinking out loud, lays the law down to Sir Toby about his drinking and the way he keeps company with a 'foolish knight'. Sir Andrew, in a stage whisper, tells the others, "That's me, I warrant you". When Malvolio immediately confirms this to be true with his next comment, Sir Andrew says triumphantly, "I knew 'twas I, for many do call me fool". The job for the actor here is to show Sir Andrew's pathetic satisfaction in his deduction. I communicated this by whispering the second line in an excited way and raising both hands to my cheeks, as if to feel the hot blush of pride spreading over them.

Task 1

Key Features
The text is the starting point of drama performance.

1. Explain why the actual words spoken by the characters are particularly crucial in drama.

2. Find the four quotations used by Mario Goodwin to show Sir Andrew is a fool.

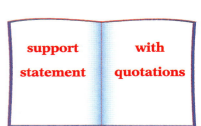

3. The quotations used in Sample One provide evidence to support the argument that Sir Andrew is a fool.

- Take a scene from the Shakespeare play that you are studying.
- Make a **statement** about **one** of the characters that you can **support** with evidence.
- Find **five short quotations** (up to around 10 words in length) that provide **evidence** to **support** your statement.

Task 2

Key Features
Any analysis of drama should show how the text will be presented in performance, and how it should affect an audience.

1. Mario Goodwin writes about the way Sir Andrew's lines were spoken and the actions that accompanied them. These things are part of stagecraft, the way that drama appears to an audience.

- Write down the **two different ways** that Sir Andrew's lines were **spoken**.
- Write down the **two actions** that went with the lines.

2. The appearance of characters is also an important part of stagecraft.

- Write a paragraph based on what you now know about Sir Andrew. Recommend how the actor playing him should appear on stage, in terms of dress, hairstyle, movement, gesture and attitude to others.

Sample Two

In this extract, Mai Wolfe writes about the importance of the 'balcony' scene in *Romeo and Juliet*. It is the scene in which Romeo, a Montague, goes to the house of his family's enemies, the Capulets, in order to see Juliet, the girl he has just fallen hopelessly in love with.

This scene is a crucial one because it really does establish the passion that exists between Romeo and Juliet. Although they have already met at the Capulets' party, what happened there was just a flirtation, something that could happen between any two young people. The fact that Romeo now returns to the Capulets' house, when it is so dangerous for him to do so, shows how deep his feelings are. We have already seen how bitter the conflict is between the Montagues and the Capulets during the fight scene at the start of the play and the aggressive behaviour of Tybalt at the party. Prince Escalus has threatened death to anyone starting another 'civil brawl' on the streets of Verona. Yet Romeo is prepared to ignore the dangers of trespassing at the home of his family's worst enemy – all for the love of Juliet.

In a dramatic sense, the scene is significant because it is so unlike the earlier action. It is obviously very different from the brawling 'bred of an airy word' that begins the play. Indeed, airy words have been very much a feature of things up until this point. Paris, the nobleman who wants to marry Juliet, expresses his love for her in a courtly way that has none of Romeo's fiery passion. Tybalt's aggressive language at the party is excessive and unnecessary, especially so after he has been ticked off by Capulet for being so hot-headed. Mercutio, above all in his 'Queen Mab' speech, talks 'of nothing'. What a contrast, then, is provided by the language and behaviour of Romeo and Juliet, pulled magnetically together by the force of their emotions. There is no pretence in their love and they speak to each other with the most powerful feelings. An audience must be made aware that this is the relationship that will drive the action of the play.

There are a number of problems a modern audience might have in truly sympathising with this scene, and I think anyone directing it must be fully aware of them. First of all, there is the language itself, which to us in the early twenty-first century may seem a little flowery. Romeo swears his love by the 'blessed moon' and both lovers make all sorts of poetic references that appear to go off the point. The best way around this problem is to ensure that the moments of humour in the scene (such as the Nurse's irritating interruptions) are brought out clearly. Perhaps even stranger to a modern audience is the age of Juliet. We know that she is 13 and that Romeo is probably not much older. The fact that they are so young and by the end of the scene are planning to get married certainly seems unusual today. There really is not much to be done about this. Most directors seem to get round the problem by ignoring it and having the actors playing Romeo and Juliet appear in their late teens.

Key Features
Comparisons within a text can improve our overall understanding of it.

1. List five references Mai Wolfe makes to other parts of the play. You could begin your list:

> ● The fight scene at the start of the play shows us that the Montagues and Capulets hate each other.

5 references

2. Take a scene from the Shakespeare play you are currently studying.

   ● Write a paragraph comparing this scene with two or three other scenes in the play.
   ● You should write about any interesting differences, but focus on quite simple elements:

   > – what **happens** in the plot
   > – contrasts in the **way people speak**
   > – the **tone/mood** created and so on.

Task 4

Key Features
References should be made to the *social* and *historical* context of the play.

It is possible that anything that seems 'odd' to you as a member of a modern audience can be written about as an element of the social and historical context.

1. In your own words, write down **two things** that Mai Wolfe thinks a modern audience might find **strange** about the balcony scene.

2. Now look back at the scene from the Shakespeare play you wrote about in (2) above. Write down **anything** in this scene that a modern audience might find **unusual** or **strange**.

Shakespeare Coursework Task

This task will involve you working in a group of between two and five members.

Choose an approximately five-minute-long section of the Shakespeare play you are studying. In your group:

- **discuss** the characters and the ideas that come across in this part of the play
- give each member of the group **at least one** character to play
- **rehearse** your part with the other members of your group
- when you are ready, **perform** the extract for the rest of the class.

Write a commentary in which you explain the elements of the drama you were trying to bring out – and the impression of your character you were trying to convey.

REMEMBER

You must include discussions (both spoken and written) of:
- language
- stagecraft (such as gesture, appearance)
- comparisons with other parts of the play
- social and historical context (what seems 'odd' to a modern audience).

MAKING THE GRADE

To get a Grade 'C' you will have to *show insight when discussing character, structure and stagecraft*. This means that you must clearly understand the personalities and motives of the characters in your scene. You need to show why they behave as they do and how you, as actors, tried to communicate your understanding to an audience.

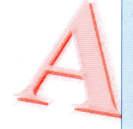

To get a Grade 'A' you will need to *show analytical and interpretative skill when evaluating* the effects of character and action. In other words you must demonstrate a very clear understanding of your characters and the means by which you used dramatic devices or **stagecraft** (such as body movements and ways of speaking) to convey this understanding to an audience.

Other Students' Work

The following three extracts are taken from assignments by Rebecca, Grant and Bethany, Year 11 students who worked together on producing Act One, Scene One of *A Midsummer Night's Dream*. The section they are writing about is the one in which Egeus is complaining to Theseus, the Duke of Athens, about the behaviour of his daughter, Hermia. She has fallen in love with Lysander against her father's wishes. Egeus wants her to marry another young man called Demetrius. Rebecca was awarded a Grade 'E' for her work, Grant a Grade 'C' and Bethany a Grade 'A'.

E Egeus was angry because Hermia decided to go off with Lysander instead of Demetrius and we saw this because Egeus said, "full of complaint come I". He thought that Lysander had tricked Hermia into loving him and he said "verses of feigning love" which means that Lysander made up poems to trick Hermia. Egeus was really angry and he shouted at Theseus so that he could get his own way, but Theseus knew he could make up his own mind anyway because he was the Duke of Athens.

C When Egeus speaks he is extremely angry with Lysander. We decided that Rebecca, who was playing Egeus, should speak her lines quickly and angrily with a raised voice. When she came to the bit about Lysander seducing Hermia with 'verses of feigning love' she looked over at Lysander (played by me) with a sneer on her face. Bethany, who was playing Theseus, stood completely still and without any expression on her face. We wanted to show the audience that the atmosphere of this part of the play is tense.

FOCUS **grade contrast**

A This is a tense moment in a generally light-hearted play. Egeus' outbreak of rage comes immediately after we see the arrangements for Theseus' and Hippolyta's wedding and he is the one who seems bad-tempered and out of place. Egeus repeats the word 'thou' when he is accusing Lysander of seducing his daughter, and Rebecca made her voice go high-pitched on the second 'thou' to indicate to the audience that the old man is not in control. She also wagged her finger in a demonstration of ineffective fury. Bethany, as Theseus, stood very still and without any expression. The intention here was to communicate Theseus' sense of annoyance at Egeus. Although he is a fellow nobleman, it would have been considered rude in Shakespeare's time for anyone to make demands on such an important character as Theseus.

NOW

- Explain the reasons why different grades have been awarded to the three students.
- Identify where Bethany has used the four key features: language, comparisons, stagecraft, context.

Sample Three   In this extract, Matt Gillespie is interviewed by Anna Kirshnan about playing the part of a character called Arthur Birling in a production of J B Priestley's play, *An Inspector Calls*.

THIS WEEK'S INTERVIEW

BY ANNA KIRSHNAN

AK What kind of man is Arthur Birling?

MG A lot of people see Birling as being 'bad' or 'wicked', but I don't agree with this analysis of him at all. He's simply very self-indulgent. He wants his business to be as successful as possible because he likes the money it brings in. He wants his daughter to marry into 'old money' because that will give his own company added status. And he wants his own family to be as comfortable as possible. There's nothing bad in any of that: it's just that while he's getting what he wants for himself he does not consider the consequences of what he's doing.

AK What do you mean by the consequences? Do you think people like Birling behaved differently to the way we behave nowadays?

MG The consequences for other people are terrible. Eva Smith commits suicide largely because Birling put her on the street. His son is a useless drunk. He doesn't know his own daughter. His prospective son-in-law is prepared to lie to him. His wife is a cardboard cut-out with no personality. All this is because Birling is so desperate for status ... so desperate to maintain appearances. I don't think people behave that differently nowadays, really. People still trample over each other and behave dishonestly to get a tiny pay rise or a slight improvement in their status. The main difference, I think, is that people now are more aware that other people are suffering because of their actions. This makes some of them feel guilty about what they may be doing – but it doesn't stop them.

AK How do you try to bring these aspects of Birling's character out on the stage?

MG You have to keep three main emotions in mind when you play Birling: complacency, anger and fear. He feels the first when he's confident at the beginning of the play; the second when the Inspector starts pushing him with his questions; the third when he realises the Inspector can expose him.

AK But how do you actually show these things to the audience?

MG Well, take the initial complacency, for example. Birling is having a few drinks with his family. You make sure that he dominates the stage. He is the one picking up the bottle of port to share around. He has the loudest laugh. He puts logs on the fire to show that he's the master of the house. He puts his hand on Gerald's shoulder to show that he is on his side. The whole sense of Birling must be that he is in control – of the port, the jokes, the fire, the company, whatever – because he's the master of the household. He's pretty pleased with that and he doesn't see anything on the horizon that's going to change it. The audience must get a real sense of Birling's self-confidence. It makes his fall later in the play much more dramatic.

Key Features

It is important to understand the characters in a play, and the way the author has characterised them.

1. Make a list of **six** of Arthur Birling's problems. You could begin:

   ● He is very self-indulgent.

2. With the evidence that you have, write a description of how you think Arthur Birling should **appear** on stage, in terms of age, height, weight, hairstyle and clothes.

● age
● height
● weight

3. Take one of the characters from the twentieth-century drama text that you are studying. Write a paragraph about the **type of person** he or she is, making sure that you provide **evidence** from the play to support your opinions.

Task 6

Key Features

Good analyses of drama always consider the text in performance.

1. Look at Matt Gillespie's fourth answer. List **four** things he did to bring out Birling's character on the stage.

2. Look again at the paragraph you wrote for Task 5, Part 3. Choose one of the scenes in which your chosen character appears and then answer the following questions.

   ● How do you think your character should **appear** on stage in this scene?
   ● What **physical actions** should they perform to bring out their **emotions** and **personality**?
   ● How should they speak some of their important lines so that they are **most effective**?

3. Read the interview with Matt Gillespie once more.

   ● Write down **four comparisons** he makes within the text.
   ● Identify the paragraph in which he refers to social and historical context.

Twentieth-Century Drama Coursework Task

Twentieth-century drama study is NOT a requirement for GCSE English; however, you could use it as a stimulus for oral work.

Choose one of the characters from the twentieth-century drama text you are studying. When you are satisfied that you fully understand your chosen character, you will be interviewed about him or her.

The more you understand your chosen character the better. If possible, watch stage or film productions of the play and act out parts of it with one or more partners.

REMEMBER

You should be prepared to answer questions on the following points:
- your character's basic **personality**
- the **actions** you think you could perform to bring out his or her personality
- the way you want your character **physically** to appear on stage
- any important **comparisons** you think can be made with your character's earlier or later behaviour in the play
- **social** and **historical** context.

MAKING THE GRADE

To get a Grade 'C' you will need to *show insight* when discussing the effects of dramatic devices. You can do this by talking about the way your staging decisions would be designed to influence an audience.

To get a Grade 'A' you will need to *show analytical and interpretative skills when evaluating the effects of dramatic devices or stagecraft.* This means that you must make specific references to the ways in which you would use particular elements of stagecraft to influence an audience's interpretation of your character.

Other Students' Work

The following extracts are taken from interviews with two students, Mairaid Loch (ML) and Danielle Trice (DT). They both chose to analyse Elizabeth Proctor from Arthur Miller's *The Crucible*. Mairaid was awarded a Grade 'D' and Danielle a Grade 'B'. They were interviewed by Roger Machin (RM).

D

RM What type of person do you think Elizabeth is?

ML Well ... she's very loyal because she doesn't try to get out of her problems by telling on her husband.

RM And ... and what else ... ?

ML She's a good Christian and she tells the other characters that she doesn't believe in witches if they think she is one.

RM How would you present her on stage?

ML She would be wearing old-fashioned clothes to show she was from those times ... I'd have her standing very still to show that she didn't really think much of her own power over other people.

B

RM What type of person do you think Elizabeth is?

DT She's a typical Puritan woman, really. She doesn't want to cause any trouble and she wants to lead a good life. She can't believe it when she's accused of being a witch because she has spent all her time trying to be really good.

RM What do you mean by a 'typical Puritan woman'?

DT Someone who did what was expected of them and always ... like ... bowed down to their husband. They didn't have as much independence as we do and their husbands expected them to do whatever they said.

RM How would you present Elizabeth Proctor on stage?

DT You need to show that she is very modest because that's a big thing in her character. You should have her talking quietly and always having her eyes looking down at the floor ... not because she's shy but because she doesn't want to be pushy. Her clothes should be very plain. They didn't have much money ... and even if they had they believed that colourful clothes were wrong and against God.

• Explain the difference between the interviews.

Unit 6 Imagine: *Original Writing Coursework/ Speaking and Listening Coursework*

In this Unit **you will read extracts from novels that describe scenes of destruction. Your Writing Coursework Task will be to imagine being in a place you know after it has been struck by a disaster. In your Speaking and Listening Task, you will debate battle tactics in an imaginary, post-nuclear world.**

Sample One

Robert Swindells' novel, *Brother in the Land*, describes the effects of a nuclear war. When the bombs drop, Danny Lodge, the teenage hero, is sheltered from the blast by an old bomb shelter on a hillside. In the following passage, Danny returns to his home town of Skipley to search for his family. Although this is an imaginary description, Swindells' plain English makes the account seem horrifyingly real.

On the edge of town the houses were all burnt out, charred, glassless windows and caved-in roofs. Inside you could see wallpaper, fireplaces and bits of stairs going nowhere. Smoke rose thinly here and there through blackened timbers.

There was this old man, sitting in an armchair on the pavement. How it got there I don't know but there he was, staring at the wet flags. He was the first living person I'd seen all the way down and I crossed over and said, "Are you all right?" It was a damn stupid thing to say but I wanted to hear his voice.

He didn't answer. He didn't even look up. He just went on staring at the pavement with his hands curled round the ends of the armrests. I repeated my question in a louder voice but there was no response; not even when I touched his shoulder. I guessed he must be in shock or something and I felt I ought to help – get him under cover perhaps. I looked about but all the houses were burnt and I couldn't see anybody else, so I left him.

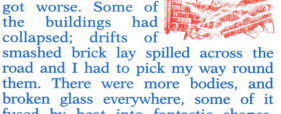

As I moved further into town the damage got worse. Some of the buildings had collapsed; drifts of smashed brick lay spilled across the road and I had to pick my way round them. There were more bodies, and broken glass everywhere, some of it fused by heat into fantastic shapes. There were burnt out vehicles and the air smelled of charred wood.

Our shop was in the west part of town, the part farthest away from Branford. The worse devastation was to the east. As I made my way westward the damage grew lighter and I began to hope that I might find my family unscathed and my home intact.

I saw people. Some were walking about. Others sat on steps, gazing at the ground in front of them. Nobody looked at me, or tried to speak. I felt invisible, like a ghost.

Task 1

Key Features
An imaginative account of an event can be made powerful by showing people's emotional reactions to it.

1. It is more effective to show what people are feeling than to tell it.
   Read these two sentences:

   > a. The old man was staring at the wet pavement.
   > b. The old man was shocked.

   - Which of the two is a '**show**' sentence and which is a '**tell**' sentence?
   - Write down other sentences from the passage that show what people are **feeling**.
   - Write down **five** sentences of your own that show: anger; happiness; jealousy; kindness; greed.

Task 2

Key Features
Imaginative writing can still be effective when it is understated.

1. There is a big difference between an **understated** style and an **exaggerated** one. Read these two sentences:

   - There was this old man, sitting in an armchair on the pavement.
   - There was this old man, slumped in an armchair, his tongue lolling out of his slavering mouth, his bloodshot eyes staring wildly as he wailed and groaned.

   understated

   exaggerated

2. Swindells has written the section you have just read in an **understated** way. Rewrite some, or all, of the passage in a **highly exaggerated** way. Use the second sentence above to give you an idea of the kind of thing you should aim for. Try to:

   - **exaggerate** the destruction that Danny sees
   - make up a **nonsense conversation** between Danny and the old man
   - describe the people walking about in **much more detail**.

3. **EXPLAIN**
   - when writing in an **understated** style is appropriate
   - when writing in an **exaggerated** style is appropriate
   - when the use of individual words, like 'slumped' and 'slavering' is appropriate.

Sample Two   In his novel *The War of the Worlds*, H G Wells describes the invasion of Earth by Martians. The following passage is an account of the destruction caused by their terrible weapons. It is seen through the eyes of the Narrator of the story as he sits looking at South London through the window of his study.

It seemed, indeed, as if the whole country in that direction was on fire – a broad hillside set with minute tongues of flame, swaying and writhing with the gusts of the dying storm, and throwing a red reflection upon the cloud scud above. Every now and then a haze of smoke from some nearer conflagration drove across the window and hid the Martian shapes. I could not see what they were doing, nor the clear form of them, nor recognise the black objects they were busied upon. Neither could I see the nearer fire, though the reflections of it danced on the wall and ceiling of the study. A sharp, resinous twang of burning was in the air.

I closed the door noiselessly and crept towards the window. As I did so, the view opened out until, on the one hand, it reached to the houses about Woking Station, and on the other to the charred and blackened pine-woods of Byfleet. There was a light down below the hill, on the railway, near the arch, and several of the houses along the Maybury road and the streets near the station were glowing ruins. The light upon the railway puzzled me at first; there was a black heap and a vivid glare, and to the right of that a row of yellow oblongs. Then I perceived this was a wrecked train, the fore part smashed and on fire, the hinder carriages still upon the rails.

Between these three main centres of light, the houses, the train, and the burning country towards Chobham, stretched irregular patches of dark country, broken here and there by intervals of dimly-glowing and smoking ground. It was the strangest spectacle, that black expanse set with fire. It reminded me, more than anything else, of the Potteries seen at night.   People at first I could distinguish none, though I peered intently for them.   Later I saw against the light of Woking Station a number of black figures hurrying one after the other across the line.

Task 3

1. The extract makes use of lots of **descriptive phrases** – containing **adjectives** – that make the narrator's vision much more dramatic or vivid. For example:

   '*... irregular* patches of *dark* country ...'

   Make a list of **10** phrases (containing adjectives) in the passage that make the description more dramatic. Underline the **adjectives**.

MAKING THE GRADE

These descriptive phrases are often known as 'noun phrases'.

2. Now choose **five** of the adjectives you have listed. Using a thesaurus, find three synonyms for each of them. Keep your new list to help you with your Coursework Task.

Task 4

1. Find examples of everyday objects that Robert Swindells and H G Wells make use of in their imaginary descriptions of destruction.

2. Make a list of at least five things you might see every day. You could include:

   - clothing
   - furniture
   - electronic items
   - jewellery
   - decorations (such as pictures)
   - toys
   - means of transport (such as bicycles)
   - items from the High Street (such as traffic lights).

5 everyday things

Save your list. It will help you with your Coursework Task.

Original Writing Coursework Task

Think about a place you like and know well. Imagine that it has been struck by a catastrophe of the kind you have read about in the extracts. As a returning survivor, you are walking around a few days after the destruction. Describe what you see.

Dos and Don'ts

REMEMBER
- express your narrator's **feelings** and **emotions** as he or she walks around the disaster scene
- show how the disaster has affected the people you describe
- write in an **understated** way: there is no need in this exercise to exaggerate
- use four or five **interesting adjectives** to make your description more vivid: you could use some of the words you listed in Task 3
- use some of the everyday objects you listed in Task 4; they should be described in unfamiliar situations around the disaster scene to create the sense that things have been dramatically disrupted.

MAKING THE GRADE

To get a Grade 'C' you will need to interest your reader by using an *appropriate style*. You must write in a way that shows the destruction of the scene without making it unbelievable.

To get a Grade 'A' you must *use vocabulary to achieve a range of original effects*. This means that you must select words with care so that they communicate a powerful sense of the destruction you are describing.

Other Students' Work

This is an extract from an assignment by Jemma. She was awarded a GCSE Grade 'E'. Her spelling and punctuation have been corrected to make the passage easier to read.

E I walked into the town and saw that everything had completely fallen to bits and there was rubbish everywhere and nobody seemed to know what was going on. One thing was that there were dead people everywhere and they had really bad injuries with blood dripping out of their bodies. All the buildings had collapsed and all I could see was stones and bricks all over the pavement. One old lady had fallen over in front of me and the bomb had blown all the windows out of the shops and there was glass everywhere. Some people were very shocked and they walked around like Zombies, dribbling out of the corner of their mouths. Some of them came towards me with their arms in front of them and they were making moaning sounds like monsters and all their clothes were ripped and torn.

FOCUS **grade contrasts**

Assessor's Comments

Jemma has described the town after the explosion but she has not done it in a convincing way. People's emotional reactions to the disaster are not shown and nor are hers. She has exaggerated the amount of destruction ('... all the buildings had collapsed') and she has not brought in the everyday objects which might have survived the blast and made her writing more dramatic. Her description of the 'Zombies' creates a cartoon effect that does not help us sympathise with the people affected by the disaster. She has included some useful adjectives. Jemma has used too many words emphasising the sameness of the scene. It would be better to have some contrast.

This is an extract from an assignment by Kyle. He was awarded a GCSE Grade 'C'.

C The city centre was deserted apart from two or three people wandering around in the ruins. As I looked at them I felt very sorry. Their clothes were grimy and black with the smoke from the explosion and they had an empty look on their faces. They did not even come near me. I walked further up the road towards Deansgate. There were still some buildings standing here. I saw a motorbike on its side in the road and a helmet resting next to it. When I walked on I saw the rider in his leathers. He had staggered away from his motorbike and now he was lying in the gutter. I was not sure if he was still alive but I did not want to stay to check. I couldn't see any injuries on him but he was lying very still and I didn't want to turn him over.

Assessor's Comments

Kyle's description is more understated than Jemma's. Although he does not talk much about the victims of the explosion, he does describe them in a way that makes us pity them. He writes about the 'empty' look on people's faces. He says that he feels 'sorry' but he could have shown his emotional reactions more through his actions. Kyle does not exaggerate the destruction. He says that there are still buildings standing in one area. He chooses an everyday object, a motorbike, and adds a nice touch by including a more personal item, the helmet, next to it. When he finds the rider, he leaves the injuries that have left him in the gutter up to the reader's imagination. The adjective 'grimy' is an unusual and interesting one, and works better than a more common adjective like 'dirty'.

Sample Three

In the following extract from *Brother in the Land*, Danny Lodge is questioned by two of his allies, Branwell and Rhodes, about the layout of a fortified farm they are about to attack. Danny knows about the farm because he has recently been a prisoner there under the brutal guard of a man called Booth.

Branwell said, "Now then, Danny: here's where your recent unpleasant experience can be turned to good use. We need to know a bit about the layout up at the Farm." He tapped the map where Kershaw Farm was shown, a cluster of minute buildings on the edge of the moor. I bent over it, wincing from the pain in my ribs.

"Well," I began, feeling daft. They were all watching me as though I was Field Marshall Montgomery or something. I tried to recall everything I'd seen during that unreal walk with Booth that might have ended in my death. "All this is surrounded by a double fence, with lights over it." I circled the Farm with my finger.

Rhodes made an impatient noise. "We know that," he snorted. "We can see that from the outside."

Branwell gave him a sharp look and said, "What about the buildings themselves, Danny? Can you tell us which buildings are used for what?"

"Hm." I chewed my swollen lip, trying to remember. "The house itself has offices in it. Rooms that have been made into offices. One is the Commissioner's office. Then there was one that said, 'Food Officer' on it, and another to do with health. There's a kitchen, and I think I heard kids upstairs somewhere." I knew I wasn't doing too well. I could feel Rhodes' sarcastic eyes on me and I flushed.

"It's all right, Danny," said Branwell. "Just take your time and try to remember. You were under a great strain at the time. We all appreciate that. What about the soldiers?"

I frowned. "There were some huts. Here, I think. They're not on the map." I pointed to an empty bit among the buildings. "They were long, and new-looking, and there were a few men in radiation-gear hanging about outside them."

Branwell nodded. "That sounds about right. Did you notice any vehicles?"

"Yes." I recalled this part vividly, and pointed to an area between the farmhouse and where the camp now was. "Here. There were some APCs, some trucks and some cars, all parked together on a concrete pad. A motorbike, too."

"Did you notice any well?" put in Rhodes. I nodded. "It's in the yard. Right by the house." I bent over the map. "Here."

Task 5

Key Features
Useful information can be communicated effectively through speech – especially to good listeners.

1. People communicate best to good listeners.

   - List three phrases that show Branwell **is a good** listener.
   - List three phrases that suggest Rhodes **is not a good** listener.

2. Danny gives Branwell and Rhodes a lot of information in this passage.

   - Write down **10** of the things Danny is able to tell the other two about Kershaw Farm.

Task 6

Key Features
Conversations (real or fictional) can tell us a lot about the people involved in them, not only by what they say, but by the way they react to what other people say.

1. The ways in which Danny, Branwell and Rhodes act, and the things they say, help us build up a picture of their personalities.

   - Write character sketches for each of the three men based on the information you have read in the extract.

Include information about:

- age
- temperament
- strengths
- weaknesses
- feelings about each other.

Speaking and Listening Coursework Task

Imagine you have survived a nuclear war. Six months have passed since the explosions. You are living with a group of 100 other survivors in terrible conditions in a ruined town. At the top of a nearby hill is the Local Control Centre (LCC) populated by heavily armed people whose aim is to destroy all opposition. Your leader, Woode, has called an urgent meeting to discuss a plan to invade the LCC and take it over. Divide yourselves into groups of three or four. Each member of the group takes one of the roles below. When you know which person you are going to be, spend 10 minutes planning how your character will contribute to the discussion. When you are ready, the character playing Woode should call the meeting and it should begin straight away, without being rehearsed.

You will need to discuss:

- arguments for and against the invasion
- the tactics to be used in an invasion
- what to do with prisoners if any are taken
- the way the LCC should be run if the invasion is successful.

JONES
A 17-year-old recently beaten up and then released from the Local Control Centre. He has important information about the strengths and weaknesses of the way the centre is organised. Even when things are going against him he remains rational and reasonable.

ARAFEH
A woman in her early 20s. She believes firmly that in the post-nuclear world all enemies should be dealt with ruthlessly. She is a skilful fighter and is respected as a military tactician. Her arguments are well thought out and the others are a little scared of her.

WOODE
The leader of the settlement. He believes that the nuclear war has made people less understanding of each other and worries that our basic humanity is being lost. His priority is to make sure that others, even enemies, are treated with dignity and respect.

PALYS
In charge of the day-to-day running of the settlement. She knows more than anyone about the basic needs and concerns of the people in the community. She believes that the settlement should put up barriers against the outside world and look after itself.

MAKING THE GRADE

To get a Grade 'C' you must *communicate ideas and issues*. This means that you express your *character's* ideas clearly, not your own ideas. You need to engage with other characters' ideas, especially their assumptions and biases.

To get a Grade 'A' you must *synthesise essential points, resolving outcomes*. You should *analyse* what others say, understanding their arguments as well as your own. Then, selecting the key points, you must present a clear case for your desired outcome.

Other Students' Work

Here is a transcript of a recording of two students involved in the same task as you. They are Sean (in role as Woode) and Basmah (as Arafeh). They are discussing what to do with prisoners if any are taken. Sean was awarded a GCSE Grade 'E'. Basmah was awarded a GCSE Grade 'A'.

Sean	So ... What ... What do you think about ... ?
Basmah	The prisoners? I think my opinion on that should be fairly obvious, Woode. These crooks have spent the last six months feeding themselves and letting the rest of Skipton starve. They've been completely ruthless. Now their time is up.
Sean	Yes, but I don't think we should be too hard on them.
Basmah	Why not, Woode? They've been hard on everyone else. They're evil and they're wicked. And you also need to think about something else. Where are we going to keep our prisoners?
Sean	There'll be places. There's a barn ... We could use one of the barns up at the farm.
Basmah	I don't want to take any prisoners. If I do, my plans will have gone wrong. What are the prisoners going to do, anyway? They'll be sat in your barn planning how to escape.
Sean	Yes. Yes, but we can't just kill them, can we?
Basmah	Listen, Woode. In this world it's a dog-eat-dog situation. How are you going to feel when one of your precious prisoners escapes and cuts one of our throats? Are you going to wait for that to happen before you do anything? We both want the same thing, and that's for good people to survive. Surely you don't want to put all our hard work at risk to protect a few traitors.

Assessor's Comments

Sean and Basmah have both stayed in role. Sean has tried to be respectful towards the rights of the prisoners and his approach is humane. His biggest difficulty, however, is that he is not behaving like a leader. He allows himself to be interrupted and does not present his arguments in a particularly convincing way. Nor does he change his arguments when he sees that those he has used are not working. He could also have developed his ideas more. For example, when he talks about putting the prisoners in a barn, he should have explained how he intended to keep them there without them escaping. Basmah, on the other hand, is very forceful and direct. She calls Woode by his name, for instance, and she justifies her wish not to take any prisoners in a number of ways. She says that they have been 'evil and wicked' so should not expect mercy from others. Her comment about them escaping shows that she is thinking about the *practical* difficulties of the situation. She asks Woode lots of rhetorical questions: by doing this she suggests that the answers are so logical and obvious that they do not need to be spoken.

Unit 7 Discuss: *Speaking and Listening Coursework*

In this Unit you will read a passage from a short story and an extract from a play. Your Coursework Task will be to discuss a real life problem. Your goal will be to reach a compromise that everyone can agree on.

Sample One

The following extract is taken from Margaret Biggs' short story, 'The Scar'. The narrator, Chris, a 14-year-old boy, is being encouraged by his English teacher, Mrs Chadwick, to take a part in the school play, *The School for Scandal*. He does not want to take the part although he has had a successful audition. He is worried about what his arm, scarred and deformed in a road accident, will look like to others when he is on stage.

"I can't do it," I gasp, not looking at her. "Forget it, choose someone else, I'm sorry but I can't."

"Hey, Chris," she says, sounding concerned. "Come here." She leads me over to a bench under a may tree. Thank heaven no one's about here. "Sit down, calm down, and tell me what's going on."

I collapse on to this bench. "I suppose you're talking about the part in *The School for Scandal*?" she says. "What's all the excitement about? You read it well, and of course you'll be able to do it, why in heaven's name not?"

"No, I can't," I repeat. "Everyone will laugh, and I don't want them to, I don't want to spoil it."

"Why should they laugh?" she says with a steely note in her voice.

"Because of my arm," I mumble.

"Your *arm*?" she says, and she sounds genuinely at a loss. "What are you talking about? What's the matter with it?"

I look up, and I can see it's not an act, she really doesn't understand. She's never noticed – it's unbelievable. "It's scarred," I have to explain. "And it's not straight. I was in an accident years ago. So you see I couldn't possibly. Look." I hold out my arm so she can see.

"That's rubbish," she says, and she sounds grim. "That's no reason at all."

"It is, it is!" I burst out.

"That's a reason for trying harder, not giving up," she says shortly.

"You don't understand," I say mournfully. "You don't know how it feels."

There's a long pause. Then she says, "I understand all right. I'll tell you something. Years ago I came off my fiancé's motorbike on a corner. You didn't know I've got an artificial leg below one knee, did you?"

I can't believe it. I just gaze at her incredulously. She's so beautiful ...

"So you see I understand all too well," she says. "But so what? We're all walking wounded if it comes to that. We've all got knocks and scars, whether people can see them or not, maybe inside us, maybe not. But that's no reason for giving up, is it?"

I feel deeply ashamed, stupid. "No," I say after a long time, looking at the clusters of daisies in the grass near my feet.

Task 1

Key Features
Differences between individual viewpoints should be brought into the discussion.

1. Before the discussion between Chris and Mrs Chadwick begins, both of them have very different points of view about the school play. Chris wants to be in it, but other people have teased him, and he is convinced he will make a fool of himself if he takes the part he has been offered. Mrs Chadwick is impressed by Chris' audition and has not even noticed his arm.

> Write two diary entries for the evening following the day of the audition. The first one is written by Chris. Try to bring out his desire to be in the play but his fear that he will look silly in front of everyone with his crooked, scarred arm. You can make up some of the details about his personal and school life so that your entry really brings out his feelings. Your second diary entry will be written by Mrs Chadwick. Show how enthusiastic she is about the play and how much she wants Chris to be in it. You will need to make up some details about both the play and Chris' acting abilities so that you can communicate her attitude.

In your separate diary entries you should try to show how the same event – the school play – is viewed in a completely different way by two people.

Task 2

Key Features
Successful discussions often reach positive outcomes.

1. At the beginning of his discussion with Mrs Chadwick, Chris has a number of negative ideas that are making him fear playing a part in *The School for Scandal*.

   Read through the passage once more. As you do so, write down a list of the arguments Chris uses for backing out of the play. You should begin with:

   - He says he 'can't do it'.

2. Now write a list of the words and phrases that show how Mrs Chadwick uses the discussion to bring about a positive outcome. Notice that it is not only what she says that is important, but how she says it. You could begin your list with:

   - She sounds 'concerned' immediately Chris starts to talk.

Sample Two

The following extract is from Arthur Miller's play, *A View from the Bridge*. Catherine, the adopted teenage daughter of Eddie and Beatrice, is talking about her plans to become a secretary. Beatrice is supporting Catherine's point of view. Eddie wants Catherine to get her typing qualifications before she goes out to work. The play is set in New York in the 1950s.

CATHERINE	Listen a minute, it's wonderful.
EDDIE	It's not wonderful. You'll never get nowheres unless you finish school. You can't take no job. Why didn't you ask me before you take a job?
BEATRICE	She's askin' you now, she didn't take nothin' yet.
CATHERINE	Listen a minute! I came to school this morning and the principal called me out of the class, see? To go to his office.
EDDIE	Yeah?
CATHERINE	So I went in and he says to me he's got my records, y'know? And there's a company wants a girl right away. It ain't exactly a secretary, it's a stenographer first, but pretty soon you get to be secretary. And he says to me that I'm the best student in the whole class –
BEATRICE	You hear that?
EDDIE	Well why not? Sure she's the best.
CATHERINE	I'm the best student, he says, and if I want, I should take the job and the end of the year he'll let me take the examination and he'll give me the certificate. So I'll save practically a year!
EDDIE	(*strangely nervous*) Where's the job? What company?
CATHERINE	It's a big plumbing company over Nostrand Avenue.
EDDIE	Nostrand Avenue and where?
CATHERINE	It's someplace by Navy Yard.
BEATRICE	Fifty dollars a week, Eddie.
EDDIE	(*to* **CATHERINE**, *surprised*) Fifty?
CATHERINE	I swear.
	Pause
EDDIE	What about all the stuff you wouldn't learn this year, though?

Task 3

1. Catherine and Beatrice use a number of facts to try to convince Eddie that taking the job is the right thing to do. Look at the list of facts below. For each fact, explain why you think either Catherine or Beatrice has mentioned it. The first one has been done for you.

- Beatrice tells Eddie that Catherine has not yet accepted the job.
  This may be so that Eddie does not feel he has been left out of the discussion. He will be more likely to agree to Catherine leaving school if he feels he has been included in the original decision making.
- Catherine says the principal called her into his office.
- The principal has told her she is the best student in the class.
- Catherine says she'll get the certificate whether she stays at school or not.
- She says she'll be working for a big plumbing company.
- Beatrice says Catherine will be earning 50 dollars a week (a good salary for a teenager in the 1950s).

NOW

- Write down two facts (one about the job itself and one about the location of the company) that Catherine does not seem eager to go into detail about. Explain why this might be.

Task 4

1. The discussion between Chris and Mrs Chadwick was one that had a positive outcome. There is no sign of that happening in this discussion.

Continue the script from the point at which it ends. Use the bullet points to help you with things Eddie might say and decide on responses from Catherine and Beatrice.

- Catherine will not be a secretary right away.
- She will be mixing with the wrong sort of people because of the location of the business.
- He had hopes for her to get a respectable, stable job, rather than one that pays a lot.
- He is still prepared to support her financially if she is willing to stay on at school.

Speaking and Listening Coursework Task

For this task you should work in groups of either two or three. Once you have decided on your group you will need to take on your roles. These are:

- a 15-year-old son or daughter
- a parent
- if you are in a group of three, another character (possibly another parent, a brother, sister, relative or friend).

When you have decided on your roles, look at the situation described below.

A 17-year-old sportsman or sportswoman has been offered the chance to go professional. They enjoy their chosen sport (you can decide which sport it is) and want the chance to be successful and make money from it. At least one of their parents, however, is opposed to the idea, saying that thousands of young people every year are kicked out of professional sport when they do not make the grade.

- Your task is to speak in role as characters (give them names), discussing solutions to this problem.

REMEMBER
- express your individual point of view clearly
- use facts as well as opinions to support your point of view
- try to reach a positive outcome.

MAKING THE GRADE

To get a Grade 'C' you will need to *make a significant contribution to the discussion.* You must be prepared to express detailed and well-argued views of the proposals.

To get a Grade 'A' you will need to *respond persuasively and engagingly.* You must show that, even if you disagree with someone else's point of view, you respect their opinion. You will need to demonstrate that you are capable of reaching compromises.

Other Students' Work

The following transcripts are from a discussion in which students talked in role about someone taking time off school to be a singer in a band. In each of the example extracts, the teenager is quoted trying to convince one of his or her parents that music is more important than education. Three samples, representing GCSE Grades 'D', 'C' and 'B', are given.

? Look, you know I've always been good at singing. This is a really good band, it's not some kind of stupid phase. We've been playing together for three years and it's not affected my school work up till now. If we can make it big we stand to bring in a lot of money and you won't be opposed to it then. If things don't work out I can always go into something else, and in any case I'm going to keep things together at school. I guarantee to you that nothing I do with the band will affect my grades. You know I've spoken to all my teachers about it and they say they can trust me ...

FOCUS

grade contrast

? I'm going to leave school whether you like it or not so there's no point arguing. I've always wanted to be a singer, you know that. You know I'm good at it as well. I could make far more money out of this than either of you two have ever made. Good rock bands make millions. If I go and work in McDonalds or behind a desk or driving a van, what future is there in that? At least I enjoy this and I'm good at it. There's no point going to school any more, anyway. I've learnt all I'm going to learn now and it's boring. It won't make any difference to my exam results ...

? OK, I completely understand your concerns and I think we need to be talking about solutions. The problem is really a fairly simple one. I want to be the lead singer in a high quality, serious band and I want to do it because I think I'm good and I think we can be successful and I love the music we play. You're both worried that if we aren't successful I'll have nothing to go back to. Let's talk about a compromise on school work. I'll get my class tutor to sign a form every week saying that I'm up to date and focused. If any of my subject teachers are not happy with my work then my form tutor won't sign the form ...

- Decide what grade was awarded to each extract.
- Now explain why the extracts have been awarded these different grades.

Unit 8 Argue: *Speaking and Listening Coursework*

In this Unit you will read an article about circuses and one about drug laws. Your Coursework Task will be to debate how money awarded to your school should be spent.

Sample One   This article is taken from a circus programme.

What sort of future can we expect for the circus in the new millennium? Indeed, is there a future in our hi-tech world for a form of entertainment with its origins in Victorian travelling menageries and freak shows? Ever since the coming of silent films the end of the circus has been prophesied, but it has shown a capacity to change and reinvent itself which has enabled it to survive for over 200 years and outlive, for example, its counterpart, the variety theatre.

At no time has that change been more marked than in the last few years. Just as the cinema killed off the hippodramas of the Victorian circus, so changes in public taste mean that animals are no longer regarded as essential to a circus performance. New elements have been tried instead, producing grungy 'chainsaw' circuses on the one hand, and super-slick theatrical shows on the other. Grunge, like punk, already seems like a passé phase with minority dissident appeal, and the sweet theatrical shows with their corporate mass marketing and not a sequin out of place will seem, to some, far too removed from the tradition of circus as raw, exciting, unpredictable entertainment.

So somewhere between these extremes lies a formula for the circus as it always has been: not for punks or ballet freaks, but for everyone regardless of age or status. And what, if any, is the role of Government in all this? Arguably, a limited one. If the circus is to be popular it should be able to stand on its own feet. The problem here is that it is not allowed to do this. VAT on admissions has a punitive effect on live entertainment and in the case of circus Britain has the highest rate in Europe, the full 17.5 per cent. All other EC countries have a reduced rate – in Spain, for example, it is seven per cent, Belgium six per cent and Ireland, zero.

At the same time, ironically, grants are handed out via the Lottery and the Arts Council with very little understanding of the circus business. For many years now, circus skills have been in severe decline in Britain (where circus originally began) so that we now rely largely on foreign artistes. There is an urgent need for money to establish genuine circus schools run and staffed by people with proven skills and experience. On recent evidence this doesn't happen. 'New Circus' has too often meant politically correct circus run by three-ball jugglers with an old bus and no experience or skills, who are subsidised to perpetuate the image of the circus as a shabby, low-skill entertainment.

Government has a role to play in the revival of the circus as vibrant popular entertainment, but its present interventions are largely misguided and counter-productive.

Task 1

1. Write down **five** of the arguments the writer is using in this article to promote the **traditional idea** of the circus. You could begin:

   ● The circus' capacity to change has enabled it to survive for over 200 years.

2. Look again at paragraphs three and four. List **three** facts the writer uses to support her arguments.

3. Write a paragraph of your own in which you argue the case for £1000 of lottery money to be given to something you support. The money could go to:

   ● a 'breakfast club' at your school
   ● an all-weather sports pitch in your neighbourhood
   ● better changing rooms at a local swimming pool
   ● a Christmas party for homeless people in your area.

   Make sure you use facts to support your argument.

   For example, *'Ten pupils in my class leave home every day without having breakfast.'*

Task 2

1. Reading through the whole article, make a list of **10** phrases used to describe the 'New Circus' and people involved with it. You could begin your list:

   ● grungy 'chainsaw' circuses

2. Explain the **effect** these phrases are meant to have.

3. Find **two** phrases the writer uses to describe the circus as she thinks it should be.

Sample Two

In the following passage, Steven Toynbee, an 18-year-old student from Leeds, argues for the legalisation of drugs.

It's always been fairly clear to me that the drugs laws in our country don't help anyone, least of all the addicts. There are a number of reasons why I believe that we should alter our attitudes in this area.

First, and most importantly, I feel that the illegality of drugs means that people who abuse them have to pay stupidly high prices. None of the most frequently used drugs – cannabis, cocaine, heroin – are expensive to produce and in many countries they grow as weeds. Why, then, do we make users pay ridiculously high prices which they cannot afford? The consequence is that they commit crime to pay for their habits. This needlessly draws innocent people into the problem.

A related problem, of course, is that those prepared to risk producing and trafficking drugs can become incredibly rich. It's obvious that people in places like Burma, Nigeria and Columbia will be tempted to make money through drugs rather than through planting agricultural crops. This leads to corruption in those countries and prevents them from developing proper economies. It is a problem that the wealthy countries of the world are contributing much towards.

By confining drug use to back rooms and alleyways, we condemn addicts to a life of criminal company and unhygienic practices such as the sharing of hypodermic syringes. If the use of drugs were legal, there would be no need for this. I firmly believe that the spread of terrible diseases like AIDS and Hepatitis B would drop rapidly if drug users felt able to come clean about their habits.

Some people are scared that the legalisation of drugs would create a 'permissive' society in which anything and everything was allowed. I strongly disagree. In countries such as Holland, where legalisation has occurred, there has been a drop in crime, not an increase. As I have already argued, this is hardly surprising, since legalisation leads to lower prices – and lower prices mean that addicts do not have to commit crimes to feed their habits.

It is clear that drug addicts are sad people with little to live for. Why punish them – and the rest of us who pay for their addiction – by making what should be cheap drugs ridiculously expensive? The obvious solution is to prescribe drugs for free to addicts. That way they are not exposed to disease, they can get help if they want it and they do not have to commit crime to finance their illness.

The arguments in favour of legalisation appear to me to be clear.

Task 3

1. Steven Toynbee frequently uses phrases that show the reader he is expressing a **personal opinion**. Read the text again and note down as many of them as you can find. You could begin with:

   > It's always been fairly clear to me ...

2. Now make **five** statements of your own expressing **your own opinion** about people begging for money. In each of your statements include one of the phrases from Steven Toynbee's article. For example:

   > It's always been fairly clear to me that we should treat beggars not as criminals, but as victims ...

Task 4

1. The article on drugs uses paragraphs to structure its arguments.

   - List the **five main arguments** in each paragraph.
   - Explain the purpose of the **first** paragraph and the **seventh** paragraph.

2. Now look back at the five statements you made in Task 3, Part 2. Use these statements as a basic structure for five paragraphs in which you express your opinion on people begging for money:

   - your five statements could be the opening sentence of each paragraph
   - add a final paragraph
   - write approximately the same amount as Steven Toynbee.

Speaking and Listening Coursework Task

£10,000

brainstorm

Your school has been awarded a £10,000 prize from an international company. The company has told your Headteacher that the money may be spent as the school likes and the Head has asked all members of the school community for suggestions on how best to do it. Your task is to decide how you think the funds should be allocated and then to argue the case for your conclusions.

- Brainstorm as many ideas as you can about how the money could be spent. Do not argue about how good the ideas are at this stage.
- Give each of the suggested items a cost.
- On your own, decide which item or items you want to prioritise.
- Make notes to support your proposed spending plan.
- Using your notes to help you, argue the case for your spending plan with the rest of the class.

! REMEMBER
- use evidence and be clear about your purpose
- make effective use of language to strengthen your arguments
- make sure your argument is properly structured.

MAKING THE GRADE

To get a Grade 'C' you will need to *be able to engage with others' ideas*. This means you must listen to what other people say and, if you disagree, tell them exactly why. You should be able to adapt, extend, support, modify or question what other people say.

To get a Grade 'A' you must *initiate and sustain discussion*. In other words you will need to be prepared to start conversations and keep them going. This will help show you are serious about considering other people's opinions and expressing your own in proper detail.

Other Students' Work

The extracts below are transcripts taken from a debate like the one you are about to have, except that the prize money of £50,000 was awarded to a small town, rather than a school. The quoted passages have been chosen to represent attainment at GCSE Grades 'E', 'C' and 'A'.

evidence to support argument

E Some of the money should be spent cleaning up the wall down at the Mill. Loads of people go there and it's really <u>disgusting to look at</u>. <u>I just think</u> it's really disgusting.

mainly the expression of opinion

recognises others' arguments

C I think <u>at least part</u> of the money should go to improving the lighting in the High Street. When you go there after dark <u>it's really dingy and shadowy</u>. It's not that people really are in danger down there. It's just that they think they are.

evidence/effective use of language

clear sense of purpose

evidence to support argument

A <u>I believe</u> that what this town needs more than anything else is better landscaping. £50,000 would buy enough trees and street furniture to completely change its appearance. <u>They did it in Lettom</u> a few years ago and it's completely changed the atmosphere there. I don't say we should spend money on <u>pretty flowers and garden gnomes</u>. They'll get trampled on and ruined in two minutes. If you have trees, solid wooden benches, wrought iron lamp posts – they look good and they'll last. <u>I'm positive</u> everyone would really appreciate it and I think it would enhance our whole living and working environment.

clear purpose

effective use of language

Unit 9   Persuade: *Speaking and Listening Coursework*

> *In this Unit* you will read two pieces of writing intended to be persuasive. Your Coursework Task will be to persuade a consumer to buy a product you have chosen to sell.

Sample One

The following advertisement is designed to persuade people of the benefits of cosmetic surgery.

CONSIDERING COSMETIC SURGERY?

Today no one has to live with physical features they are unhappy with, but deciding to change the way you look is not something you undertake lightly. If you are considering cosmetic surgery then you will want to know you're in safe hands from the beginning to the end. You will want the services of a fully accredited Consultant Surgeon and Anaesthetist, backed by a skilled, caring professional nursing team and a top quality, well established private hospital offering a comprehensive range of support services and after care.

The Kings Oak Hospital is a modern private hospital in Enfield, operated by BMI Healthcare, the country's leading independent healthcare provider. Here you will find that your consultant is a fellow of the Royal College of Surgeons and is also likely to be a member of The British Association of Plastic Surgeons, The British Association of Aesthetic Plastic Surgeons or another relevant specialist professional organisation.

Originally only undertaken by celebrities and the very wealthy, advancements in cosmetic surgery have resulted in lower prices making it available to people in all walks of life. Besides the 'traditional' operations for women there's a growing number of men undertaking all types of cosmetic surgery.

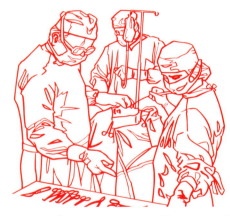

Most cosmetic surgery procedures require a general anaesthetic, but remember, every person is unique and the same operation will have different results on different patients. The variable healing qualities of people make it difficult to give exact recovery periods. Some patients bruise easily and take longer to heal whilst pain tolerance differs greatly with individuals. The time you need to take away from work will depend on the operation and your occupation.

You are advised to discuss your wish for cosmetic surgery with your GP and ask to be referred to an accredited and reputable Plastic Surgeon. This will give you the opportunity to meet with the Consultant Surgeon, briefly discuss your requirements and view the hospital if you wish. At this initial consultation you will be given advice and information, and should you decide to progress further, you will need to have a full consultation with the Surgeon before undergoing any operation.

Task 1

Key Features
Persuasive language plays an important part in advertisements.

1. Make a list of at least **five** words and short phrases that are used to present the Kings Oak Hospital in the most positive way. Your list could begin:

   in safe hands

2. Look through the list you have just made and underline the adjectives.

   You will want the services of a <u>fully accredited</u> Consultant Surgeon and Anaesthetist ...

3. Now remove the adjectives from the phrases that contain them.

   You will want the services of a Consultant Surgeon and Anaesthetist ...

   What is the effect of this?

4. This advertisement also uses language to make the reader feel as if he or she is being talked to in a polite, but personal and friendly way. Write down three examples that show this.

Task 2

Key Features
Persuasive texts have a clear purpose.

1. Write down as clearly as you can what you think the **purpose** of the Kings Oak advertisement is.

2. Make a list of at least **five** other situations in which persuasion is required. You could start with:

   ● persuading a friend to see a film with you that they say they're not interested in.

3. Now choose one of the situations you listed in 2 above. Write down **five** things you could say to persuade the other person/people to do as you want them to. For example:

   Apparently, there's a really funny scene right near the end when ...

Sample Two   The extract below is taken from a Health Education Authority publication about pregnancy. It is designed to persuade pregnant women that a healthy diet is important.

YOUR HEALTH IN PREGNANCY

A healthy diet is an important part of a healthy lifestyle at any time, but particularly if you are pregnant or are planning a pregnancy. Eating healthily during pregnancy will help your baby develop and grow and will help keep you fit and well.

- **Eat plenty of fruit and vegetables** as these provide the vitamins and minerals, as well as fibre which helps digestion and prevents constipation. Eat them lightly cooked in a little water or raw to get the most out of them. Frozen, tinned and dried fruit and vegetables are good too.

- **Starchy foods like bread, potatoes, rice, pasta, chapatis, yams and breakfast cereals** are an important part of any diet and should, with vegetables, form the main part of any meal. They are satisfying, without containing too many calories, and are an important source of vitamins and fibre. Try eating wholemeal bread and wholegrain cereals when you can.

- **Lean meat, fish, poultry, eggs, cheese, beans and pulses** are all good sources of nutrients. Eat some every day.

- **Dairy foods, like milk, cheese and yoghurt** are important as they contain calcium and other nutrients needed for your baby's development. Choose low-fat varieties wherever possible. You can get seven pints of milk free per week if you are on Income Support or income-based Jobseeker's Allowance.

- **Try to cut down on sugar and sugary foods** like sweets, biscuits and cakes and sugary drinks like cola. Sugar contains calories without providing any other nutrients the body needs. It also adds to the risk of tooth decay.

- **Cut down on fat and fatty foods as well**. Most of us eat far more fat than we need. Fat is very high in calories and too much can cause excess weight gain and increase the risk of heart disease and it can contribute to being overweight. Avoid fried foods, trim the fat off meat, use spreads sparingly and go easy on foods like pastry, chocolate and chips which contain a lot of fat. Choose low-fat varieties of dairy products, for example semi-skimmed or skimmed milk, low-fat yoghurt and half-fat hard cheese.

- **Have drinks which contain caffeine – coffee, tea and colas – in moderation**, as there may be a slight risk that too much caffeine will affect your baby's birthweight. Try decaffeinated tea and coffee, fruit juice or mineral water.

Task 3

1. Write down **five** of the **benefits** to be gained from following the dietary advice that is given in the passage. Your list could begin:

   ● Eating healthily will help a baby develop and grow.

2. Now choose something you do (or something you would like to do). Write a list of **five benefits** designed to persuade someone else to take up the activity. For example:

> judo – gives you confidence
> computer games – help your reflexes

Task 4

1. List **six** of the negative consequences of a bad diet.

2. Imagine you are the manufacturer of a low-fat, low-sugar variety of yoghurt called YoLite. Using some of the information contained in the extract, write an advertisement for your product directed at pregnant women. You could begin:

   If you are pregnant you will want the best for yourself and your baby. YoLite Yoghurt has all the benefits of traditional dairy products and none of the drawbacks.

3. What are the differences between your advertisement and the information in the original article? What are the reasons for the differences?

Speaking and Listening Coursework Task

Your company has designed and manufactured a new product. You believe it will have real benefits. Your task is to persuade a consumer to buy the product.

First you will need to decide on what your new product will be. Choose one of the following:

- a cat pushchair
- new computer software
- food that improves your IQ
- a mobile rodent catcher
- a product to help the elderly in their homes.

Make brief notes on how you will sell your product to a consumer, who will be either your teacher or another member of the class.

As a consumer, list three questions you could ask about each of the above products. Be prepared to ask new questions that occur to you during your discussion.

Give your presentation, and respond to the questions other people ask.

! **REMEMBER**
- **invent** as much **detail** as you can about your product
- provide **lots** of **information**
- be **certain** of the **benefits** of using it
- work out some of the **negative consequences** of not using it.

MAKING THE GRADE

To get a Grade 'C' you will need to *be able to promote a point of view*. This means you must be as persuasive as you can be about the product you are selling.

To get a Grade 'A' you will need to *respond persuasively and engagingly*. In other words, you must answer your consumer's questions in a way that really makes them feel your product is vital for them.

Other Students' Work

The following three passages show answers that were graded at GCSE 'F', 'C' and 'A'. All three students, in role as sales staff, were trying to persuade the target consumer (a pregnant woman) to buy the YoLite yoghurt you read about in Task 4. In each case, the students are answering the same question: 'Why is YoLite different from other yoghurts?'

Read the notes to see why the responses were graded differently.

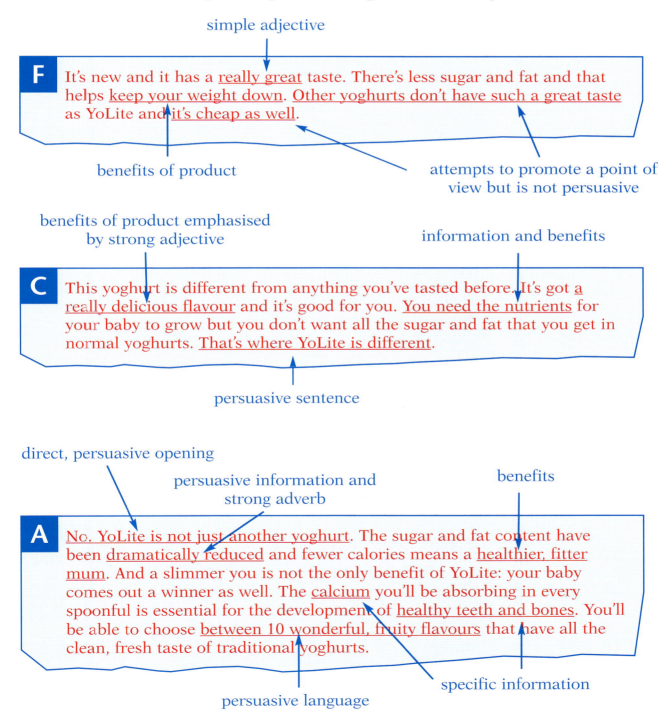

simple adjective

F It's new and it has a <u>really great</u> taste. There's less sugar and fat and that helps <u>keep your weight down</u>. <u>Other yoghurts don't have such a great taste</u> as YoLite and <u>it's cheap as well</u>.

benefits of product

attempts to promote a point of view but is not persuasive

benefits of product emphasised by strong adjective

information and benefits

C This yoghurt is different from anything you've tasted before. It's got <u>a really delicious flavour</u> and it's good for you. <u>You need the nutrients</u> for your baby to grow but you don't want all the sugar and fat that you get in normal yoghurts. <u>That's where YoLite is different</u>.

persuasive sentence

direct, persuasive opening

persuasive information and strong adverb

benefits

A <u>No. YoLite is not just another yoghurt</u>. The sugar and fat content have been <u>dramatically reduced</u> and fewer calories means a <u>healthier, fitter mum</u>. And a slimmer you is not the only benefit of YoLite: your baby comes out a winner as well. The <u>calcium</u> you'll be absorbing in every spoonful is essential for the development of <u>healthy teeth and bones</u>. You'll be able to choose <u>between 10 wonderful, fruity flavours</u> that have all the clean, fresh taste of traditional yoghurts.

specific information

persuasive language

Unit 10 Entertain: *Original Writing Coursework*

In this Unit

you will read extracts from two novels: *Jane Eyre,* by Charlotte Brontë, and *Seduction,* by Charlotte Lamb. You will focus on the way relationships between men and women are expressed in both passages. In your Coursework Task, you will write an extract from a romance.

Sample One

In *Jane Eyre* Charlotte Brontë tells the story of a penniless but dignified girl who acts as governess for a wealthy, rugged gentleman, Mr Rochester. In time, Mr Rochester falls in love with Jane and asks her to marry him. The following passage, told from Jane Eyre's point of view, describes events the morning after Mr Rochester's proposal.

"Come and bid me good morning," said he. I gladly advanced; and it was not merely a cold word now, or even a shake of the hand that I received, but an embrace and a kiss. It seemed natural: it seemed genial to be so well loved, so caressed by him.

"Jane, you look blooming, and smiling, and pretty," said he: "truly pretty this morning. Is this my pale, little elf? Is this my mustard-seed? This little sunny-faced girl with the dimpled cheek and rosy lips; the satin-smooth hazel hair, and the radiant hazel eyes?" (I had green eyes, reader; but you must excuse the mistake: for him they were new-dyed, I suppose.)

"It is Jane Eyre, sir."

"Soon to be Jane Rochester," he added: "in four weeks, Janet; not a day more. Do you hear that?"

I did, and I could not quite comprehend it: it made me giddy. The feeling the announcement sent through me, was something stronger than was consistent with joy – something that smote and stunned: it was, I think, almost fear.

"You blushed, and now you are white, Jane: what is that for?"

"Because you gave me a new name – Jane Rochester; and it seems so strange."

"Yes, Mrs Rochester," said he; "young Mrs Rochester – Fairfax Rochester's girl-bride."

"It can never be, sir; it does not sound likely. Human beings never enjoy complete happiness in this world. I was not born for a different destiny to the rest of my species: to imagine such a lot befalling me is a fairy tale – a day-dream."

"Which I can and will realise. I shall begin today. This morning I wrote to my banker in London to send me certain jewels he has in his keeping – heirlooms for the ladies of Thornfield. In a day or two I hope to pour them into your lap: for every privilege, every attention shall be yours that I would accord a peer's daughter, if about to marry her."

Task 1

1. Write a list of **six** nice things Mr Rochester says to and about Jane. Start the list with:

   He says she looks 'blooming and smiling and pretty'.

2. Now write a list of between **five** and **10 compliments** of your own in the style of Mr Rochester. Try to make at least some of your praise a little exaggerated. Look at the way the following example is developed.

   My mouse!

   My sweet mouse!

   You are my sweetest little chocolate mouse!

   Keep your list. You will need it for the Coursework Task.

3. Explain what Mr Rochester's comments show about his attitude towards Jane, apart from the fact that he loves her.

Task 2

1. Use a thesaurus to look up **two synonyms** for each of the words on the clipboard. They are different adjectives to describe the way Jane may be feeling. Choose synonyms for them that fit with a **romantic** theme. Keep your list to help you with your Coursework Task.

- blissful
- joyful
- wonderful
- heavenly
- perfect

2. Write down **three** pieces of evidence that demonstrate Mr Rochester's **decisiveness**.

3. Write down **three** pieces of evidence that show Jane has **less authority** than Mr Rochester.

Sample Two

The following passage is taken from the novel *Seduction* by Charlotte Lamb. Clea, the heroine of the story, has been swimming in the sea. When she comes out to dry herself she encounters Ben, who has come down to the beach in his car. He wants to drive her away with him.

Clea walked on towards the gate which let her out onto a stony, dusty lane. Beyond that the beach began ...

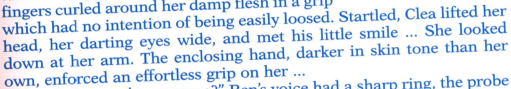

She swam for ten minutes, enjoying the salty spray which the wind flung into her face ... When she came out of the sea, she halted in surprise ...

Ben was on his feet before she had turned away, his hand grabbed her arm, his fingers curled around her damp flesh in a grip which had no intention of being easily loosed. Startled, Clea lifted her head, her darting eyes wide, and met his little smile ... She looked down at her arm. The enclosing hand, darker in skin tone than her own, enforced an effortless grip on her ...

"Why won't you come?" Ben's voice had a sharp ring, the probe of his eyes fierce ...

"Will you let go of my arm, please. You're hurting!"

His fingers tightened rather than slackened, the grey eyes turning darker, filling with impatience. "No, I'm not hurting you!"

He hadn't been, it was true, but now he was, and she sensed that he was doing it deliberately, his fingers biting into her. She looked down, trying to control a strange trembling which had begun inside her, in the pit of her stomach, as though she had swallowed a butterfly which was trying to escape ...

He opened the door of his white car as if to get into it, and Clea began to turn away. Hands fastened around her waist and she gave a muffled cry as she was swung up and round, deposited like a doll inside the car. Before she could get out again Ben was beside her in the driver's seat, the engine starting with a roar. Clea fumbled angrily at the handle as the car soared into flight, but Ben's arm shot out sideways and slapped her hands down from the handle.

"Let me out!"

"Sit still, and don't be a little idiot!"

She drew herself into a tight little corner, her eyes smouldering. "You had no right to do this!"

"What have rights got to do with it? You wanted to come."

"I did not!"

"Oh, yes, you did," he mocked, his dark lashes covering his eyes yet leaving her with the distinct impression that he was watching her through them. "You wanted to come as much as I wanted to take you."

Task 3

Key Features
Conflict between characters is an important part of interesting the reader in fiction.

1. Rewrite the paragraph beginning 'He opened the door of his white car ... '
   Change the gender of the characters so that Clea and Ben are switched
   with each other. Your new paragraph should begin: 'She opened the door
   of her white car ...'

2. Explain the effect this gender switching has had.

3. Do you think Clea (in the original text)

a. wants Ben to leave her alone	b. wants Ben to overpower her?

   Explain the reasons for your choice.

Task 4

Key Features
Setting is an important feature of fiction.

1. Explain why the **setting** of this passage is appropriate for a **romantic**
   theme.

2. Write a list of **five** other **settings** that would work for **romances**.

3. Look at how you can develop a simple sentence to describe the effect of
   a setting feature (the wind) on a romantic heroine:

> Simple sentence: The wind blew her hair.
>
> Development: The *gentle breeze played with* her hair.
>
> Further development: The gentle breeze *rustled through the leaves overhead* and played with her hair.
>
> Final sentence: **The gentle breeze rustled through the leaves overhead and played teasingly with her thick, dark hair.**

4. Now write one sentence, developed in a similar way to the last one, for
   each of the features below, to show the effect they might have on a
   romantic hero or heroine.

● sand	● trees	● a river	● grass	● rain

Original Writing Coursework Task

Either

Write an extract from a romantic novel (that you have made up) using the same style as the passages you have read.

Or

Write a parody that makes the romantic style look silly. You can do this by exaggerating your writing so that it cannot be taken seriously. Make sure you select a situation that is not at all romantic. This will make your exaggerated language more out of place and funnier. The example below will help you.

His dark animal eyes gleaming with strange passion, Tarquin walked with stealthy purpose towards Jemima. He stopped at arm's length, even he not daring at this stage to advance further. "My darling," he whispered: "I think I have hardly ever seen you looking so beautiful." He placed the tea towel on the counter to conceal a forgotten splodge of lunchtime's tomato ketchup. As he did so, the wind blew through the open window and rustled his wavy hair. Not taking his eyes from Jemima, he murmured, "I've taken the cod in parsley sauce out of the freezer for later. Will you be tempted?" As he spoke, a mighty crash of thunder split the air …

Before you begin to write you will need to decide on:

- names for your romantic hero and heroine
- where your extract is going to be based
- a conflict between the two of them
- how setting features will affect the lovers.

REMEMBER
- include some of the compliments you wrote down in Task 1
- your heroine should be emotional
- your hero should be decisive.

Features two and three above are elements of this type of writing, not of real life. If you are writing a parody, you could switch the gender as you did in Task 3. The effect might be a comic one.

MAKING THE GRADE

To get a Grade 'C' you will need *to develop characters and settings*. In other words, your characters must be described as fully as possible in a romantic way. Your setting should affect the characters and add to the overall romantic atmosphere.

To get a Grade 'A' you will need *to use vocabulary to achieve original effects*. This means that you must choose interesting, individual words that bring out the romantic theme of your story extract. The sentences in Task 4 contain words that do this.

Other Students' Work

The following three extracts are all the work of one student, Naomi, who was taking part in a writing workshop. The spelling and punctuation have been corrected to make the passages easier to read.

First of all, Naomi read the extract from Charlotte Lamb's *Seduction*. Then, without any further help, she was asked to write a passage in the same style. This is part of what she wrote.

D Kyle was a very handsome man. He had dark hair and a strong chin. His eyes were light green and he had beautiful white teeth. He was sitting in the car opposite Beth. He leaned towards her. He really did love her and he knew he did more than anything else in the world. "Will you marry me?" he said. He felt like he was going to die if she said no. There was nothing else in the world he wanted more than to make Beth his wife and for her to have his children.

Next, Naomi was given the whole of the unit you have just worked through and asked to rewrite her extract. The section above now came out like this.

B Kyle was so handsome. His face was dark and mysterious but his light green eyes made him seem almost playful. As he sat in the car, Beth had to struggle to keep her emotions under control. The sun outside beat through the windscreen and a bead of sweat formed on Kyle's forehead. He loved Beth so much. "Will you marry me?" he murmured, fearing that he would die if she said no. With all the passion in his heart he wanted to make Beth his wife and bear his children.

Finally, Naomi spoke to her teacher about the work. She was given further advice about how to improve the passage. This is what she wrote.

A Beth glanced sideways at Kyle, hardly daring to look at him for more than a second. He was so handsome. Although he was dark and mysterious, his light green eyes made him seem almost playful. The passions rose within her and she struggled to contain them. After all, she had been married to Richard, her childhood sweetheart, for only six months. What would he think if he could even see her alone with Kyle, let alone know what she was thinking? The sun outside beat through the windscreen and a bead of sweat formed on Kyle's forehead. He loved Beth so much. If only that fool Richard had not come between them. Kyle's breath came more quickly and he spoke before he knew it. "Beth! Come away with me! Nobody need know where we've gone." With all the passion in his heart he wanted Beth. He wanted to take her away.

● Explain how Naomi's writing improves.

Unit 11 Review: *Media Coursework*

In this Unit you will read extracts from two reviews that appeared in a national newspaper. Your Coursework Task will be to write your own review of a film or television programme.

Sample One   The following review is of the film *The Next Best Thing*.

Beware any film that ends by thanking a swami for 'illuminating the meaning of yoga'. As all those who have watched thousands of American movies know, good, honest trash is invariably more fun – and generally more enlightening – than mediocre homilies with high-minded intentions. When Hollywood hops up on its soap box, it's time to take a powder.

The Next Best Thing (12) starts out as a sort of screwball comedy. Madonna plays Abbie, a yoga instructor with permanent man trouble; Rupert Everett is Robert, a gardener and her gay confidant. Their unconventional friendship is tested after they topple into bed one drunken evening (shot, bizarrely, as a Thirties musical fantasy), an event that leaves her with child. They form a family unit in which he will perform all the traditional functions of a father and husband, "including", as one of Abbie's friends pithily observes, "not sleeping with you".

Six years pass, apparently without further mishap, until Abbie starts dating again. Her new chap (Benjamin Bratt) seems personable enough, although you suspect from the start he's bad news when he prefers Frank (Sinatra) to Judy (Garland), cheats his way to a table at a busy restaurant and, worst of all, turns out to be an investment banker from back East.

When he proposes, the scene is set for a custody struggle in which Abbie has no qualms about surrendering her New Age principles to a homophobic attorney, and Robert finds that, for all the efforts of the gay rights movement, he is soon enough disenfranchised by the justice system.

The film is well-meaning, it tackles interesting issues, it deals thoughtfully with the compromises required of those who would defy social convention. But it's a bore. The secondary characters, including the all-important little boy, are ciphers, but even Madonna demonstrates again her lack of screen charisma when not permitted to sing or wear snazzy frocks.

Meanwhile, Everett, a far cry from the droll charmer he played in *My Best Friend's Wedding*, is required to spend so much time brooding, throwing hissy fits and taunting Abbie's lovers, that it's hard to side with him when he emerges as the hero of the piece.

Sheila Johnston

ciphers = codes/symbols carrying little value

swami = religious teacher

homilies = sermons

pithily = to the point

Task 1

1. Count and note down the **number of sentences** in each of the paragraphs. When you have done this, **explain possible reasons** for what you have found.

2. Read again the first two sentences of the fifth paragraph. Explain the **effect** of having such a **long sentence** followed by one of only a **few words**.

3. Paragraphs three, five and six use a variation of what is often called '**the rule of three**'. Find out where Sheila Johnston has done this and then explain **why** it is effective.

4. Many reviews use '**asides**' directed towards the reader. These are signalled either by the use of dashes or brackets. Write down **all the asides** that Sheila Johnston uses in this review. Explain **why** you think they are there in each case.

Task 2

1. Read all six paragraphs once more. Three of them express Sheila Johnston's **opinions**. Use the opinions expressed in these paragraphs to answer the following questions.

   - Why does Sheila Johnston find Hollywood films like *The Next Best Thing* so irritating?
   - What is Johnston's opinion of the 'secondary' actors?
   - What, according to the reviewer, are Madonna's weaknesses as an actress?
   - Why does Johnston find it difficult to see Robert as an heroic figure?

2. Look again at the second and fifth paragraphs.

   - Find one **opinion** expressed in the second paragraph.
   - In your own words, write down the **two opinions** expressed in the first two sentences of the fifth paragraph.

Sample Two

The following review is of a *Panorama* programme made during the England soccer team's unsuccessful campaign at the 2000 European Championships. The documentary followed a group of England supporters as they travelled to Belgium.

LAST NIGHT'S TV

My only regret about England being knocked out of Euro 2000 is that we will no longer be seeing Michael Owen's advert for the Nationwide Building Society. Nothing in recent weeks has caused me as much amusement as this. Prompted by his fellow footballer, Garth Crooks, Owen stares into the camera and intones his piece about the Nationwide's gorgeous terms and conditions. Heroically uninflected, devoid of any variation in tone, it sets a new benchmark for wooden delivery that will stand for years.

No doubt Owen is a genius compared to the vast majority of England football fans seen in *Panorama Special: England's Shame* (Tuesday BBC1). Reporter Gavin Hewitt followed three fatties from Newcastle as they journeyed to Belgium for last weekend's game against Germany in Charleroi. On the ferry over they showed one another their beer bellies and playfully tried to force one man's big bald head into his solar plexus. "It's raucous at times," noted Hewitt nervously, "but good-humoured."

On arrival in Belgium, Fatty Steve was hugely indignant about being stopped and searched by the police. "Outrageous," he huffed. Meanwhile in Charleroi itself, other English numbskulls were already shouting abuse and tossing furniture about. Their level of stupidity can be gauged from the fact that they were chanting "No surrender to the IRA" at a group of understandably bemused-looking Belgians.

Soon, of course, a full-scale riot was underway, led and co-ordinated by known troublemakers easily identified by the *Panorama* team – the much-vaunted safeguards to stop hooligans from travelling plainly having proved useless. A weedy liberal about so much else in life, I find a red haze of fury coming over me at the sight of more football violence.

All last week I idly devised suitable punishments for those responsible. Spraying them with indelible dye mixed with some massive skin irritant has been my most favoured option to date – although at times like this, selective amputation takes on a particular allure.

The only solace to be gained from this is that the Belgian police laid about them with commendable gusto. In the end, denied any Belgians, Turks or Germans to taunt, the English hooligans turned on each other. Brave men and worthy patriots! Just before the final credits, a Home Office minister called Lord Bassam popped up to say in patrician tones, "I think there is perhaps a lacuna in the legislation." That's no lacuna, chum, that's a gaping void.

John Preston

---

patrician = noble, refined

lacuna = gap or space

gusto = vigour, energy

Task 3

Key Features
A review may sometimes focus more on what is being shown than on how it is presented.

1. In Sample One, Sheila Johnston is critical of how the film *The Next Best Thing* has been made. In Sample Two, John Preston talks about what he has seen on television. He is not criticising the programme makers. Read through the passage again and answer the following questions.

   - What is Michael Owen being criticised for in the first paragraph?
   - What three things described in the third paragraph does John Preston find stupid about the fans?
   - In what way is the fifth paragraph different from the others?

2. Identify the paragraphs in which the following time markers appear.

   Explain how these words and phrases help the reader.

Task 4

Key Features
Critics often use rudeness for comic effect.

1. Write a list of six things or people that John Preston invites us to laugh at.

2. Explain how John Preston uses humour against

   - the England soccer team
   - hooligans
   - himself

Media Coursework Task

Decide whether you want to review a film or a television programme. When you have made your decision, read the notes below. They will help you to structure your writing.

If you are reviewing a film:

- spend half your review summarising the film in an interesting way
- in the other half of the review you should express your opinions on the acting
- try to use some of the style features (for example, the 'rule of three') you identified in Task 1
- if your review is negative, use humour for effect.

If you are reviewing a TV programme:

- choose a documentary or a non-drama programme to review
- spend most of your review expressing opinions on programme content, rather than how the programme has been made
- use some of the time markers you identified in Task 3
- if your review is negative, try to use humour (perhaps even rudeness?) for effect.

MAKING THE GRADE

To get a Grade 'C' you will need to be able *to present and explain opinions*. So when you write your review you must clearly express your own thoughts and feelings about what you have seen.

To get a Grade 'A' you will need *to express ideas coherently, logically and persuasively*. This means that you need to give a full and detailed account of what you have seen so that the reader understands clearly what you are writing about. You must persuade the reader through your language and knowledge that your opinions are valid.

Other Students' Work

Here are the opening paragraphs from two reviews of a film called *Falling Down*. The first student, Carina, was awarded a Grade 'D'. The second student, Sammy, was given a Grade 'B'.

D | *Falling Down* stars Michael Douglas and Robert Duvall. William Foster (Douglas) has recently been sacked from his job but he has not told any one else about it because he is ashamed. He drives out from his mother's home every morning (he lives with her even though he is in his late thirties) and pretends to go to the office. When the movie opens, he is sitting in a traffic jam getting annoyed by things like: a fly, the traffic, the heat, the noise and people swearing. He loses his temper and gets out of the car in a fury, leaving it in the middle of the road. After this, he goes to a shop to get change for a phone call to his ex-wife. The store keeper will not give it to him, so Foster smashes up his shop.

B | I'm not a fan of Michael Douglas or of Robert Duvall but both of them give good performances in Joel Schumacher's *Falling Down*. Douglas plays William Foster, a thirty-something recluse with a nerdy respect for authority and the 'American Way'. When he loses his job he becomes unbalanced and starts to attack the attitudes and institutions that he blames for selling out both himself and his country. What starts out as a spat in a traffic jam and a row with a shop keeper quickly turns into a homicidal rampage through the streets of Los Angeles complete with a gym bag full of guns and a rocket launcher. Prendergast (Duvall) is the cop who has to stop Foster before he gets to his ex-wife and child.

- Explain why Sammy has been awarded a higher grade than Carina.

The following extract is from a review of a travel programme by Anna, a Year 10 student.

B | This week, TravelAsia went to Kuala Lumpur, or KL as it is more commonly known. Dinusha Afzal went in for all the usual presentational gags, popping up like a glove puppet to taste the local food or point out an interesting building. KL has some of the most interesting buildings in the world. The Petronas Towers are now the tallest two man-made constructions on Earth, although the embarrassed tourist guide was forced at one point to admit that the office space still was not all rented out. KL is also one of the most polluted cities in Asia, a major achievement when you consider the competition. It might be something to do with all the old cars we saw speeding past the choking cameraman. I'm not sure Afzal should have been quite so eager to sample the food off the street sellers with all those exhaust fumes around.

- Anna's review was awarded a Grade 'B'. Read the Assessor's notes below to see why.

Anna has used an appropriately informal style. She gives readers 'inside information' like telling them that Kuala Lumpur is 'more commonly known' as KL. Her writing gives us the sense that there is a real human being behind her pen. She points out, for example, that the tourist guide was 'embarrassed' and she uses humour to draw our attention to Dinusha Afzal ('a glove puppet') and the pollution in KL, which is so bad it is almost an 'achievement'. The weakest element of this extract is Anna's organisation. She tries to link together too much loosely related information. She should have used short paragraphs that focused on separate parts of the programme, such as the buildings, pollution and food.

Unit 12 Comment: *Media Coursework*

In this Unit you will read comments on two different advertisements. Your Coursework Task will be to comment on how a magazine advertisement is attempting to sell its product.

Sample One   In this passage, Hannah McTeague comments on a magazine advertisement for Breitling watches.

The visual appearance of this advert is extremely important. A woman's diamond-studded Breitling dominates the whole page. It is the most significant feature and it suggests that the product is so beautiful and majestic it can stand on its own without other visual props. The hands of the watch stand symmetrically at ten past ten as if to emphasise the stability and order the wearer will enjoy if she chooses this product. About three-quarters of the background is taken up with a picture of the sky at dawn. The sun is just visible rising above the horizon into a dark blue and cloudless sky. The suggestion may be that the wearer of a Breitling looks forward to each new day with 'unclouded' energy and enthusiasm because she is dynamic and confident. Across the top of the dawn sky there is visible the jet stream of an aeroplane. This reminds the reader of Breitling's proud claim to be the watch worn by more international pilots than any other. In the bottom right-hand corner, the Breitling logo, a decorative 'B' flanked with wings, reinforces the theme of aviation. Obviously, Breitling hopes to benefit from the aviation industry's reputation for precision and reliability as well as glamour.

The language of the advert emphasises the ideas communicated by the visual images. The header reads 'Sheer elegance can go hand in hand with an unerring taste for precision and sturdiness'. The idea here is that things that are reliable do not have to be ugly. The beauty and status of the watch is confirmed in the first three words of the text: 'Luxury. Class. Prestige.' These words stand alone as sentences as if to say that Breitling are so confident of the truth of what they are claiming there is no need for anything else to be said. The theme of high status is continued throughout the advertisement. Breitling watches are referred to as 'chronographs'. The attractive design of the watch is called its 'aesthetic appeal'. When the advert talks specifically about the watches Breitling makes for women they are labelled 'Wings Lady'. The wrong impression would be created if they were called 'Wings Women'!

Breitling's links with aviation continue to be mentioned throughout the text of the advert. The word 'aviation' is mentioned three times as a reminder of the reliability the wearer of a Breitling enjoys. Other phrases, like 'technical perfection', 'precision and reliability criteria' and 'chronometer certification' all suggest a rigorous testing programme through which these watches must go. The idea that a 'Wings Lady' can have it all is summed up in the closing words that claim Breitling offers a 'blend of utter elegance and high performance'.

Task 1

1. Read the first paragraph again. List **five visual features** of the Breitling advert. Then do a quick, outline sketch of the **layout/look** of the advert, as described in Hannah's piece.

2. Make a list of **five conclusions** Hannah McTeague comes to about these visual features.

3. Find three magazine advertisements of your own. List details of any **interesting visual features**. Then write down your **conclusions** about these features.

Task 2

1. Hannah McTeague focuses on words and phrases she believes Breitling have chosen to emphasise the quality and reliability of their product.

   - Write down a list of five of these words and phrases.

2. Imagine you are marketing a far cheaper watch than the Breitling but that you still want to emphasise attractiveness and reliability. Make a list of words and phrases which could be used for this purpose. You could begin:

   - a price that's good for you
   - stylish

   - outstanding performance

   You could use some of the words from the Breitling advertisement as the starting points for a thesaurus search.

3. Write a 100-word advertisement for a cheap and reliable watch that seems to offer the same as the Breitling. Use some of the words and phrases you thought of in the exercise above.

In this passage, Leon O'Driscoll comments on audience and information in a magazine advertisement for a Toyota Yaris.

THE TOYOTA YARIS

The Toyota Yaris is a relatively small car, a fact that probably would not worry a lot of drivers. Toyota, however, spend a lot of the advert for the Yaris talking about its size. This suggests that the audience they are trying to reach might see its smallness and lack of power as a problem. Just look at the evidence. The background picture – the image to which the viewer's attention is immediately drawn – is of a bee whizzing through a tear it has made (impossibly, of course) in a plastic fly swat. Above this fantasy photograph, a header text asks the question 'How can small be powerful?' The opening lines of the main text point out that although small cars are not usually powerful, the 'new Yaris SR doesn't follow the rules'. What does all this evidence tell us about the intended audience? Probably that Toyota are making a play for a youngish group of people who fear that their street cred might suffer if they are seen in a car that looks more appropriate for the visit of a middle-aged shopper to Sainsbury's. The idea that the Yaris breaks rules and 'defies logic' also seems to be designed to appeal to a youthful audience who are often said to be impatient with rules and the established ways of doing things.

The information Toyota provide with the advert generally backs up the sense that they are targeting an audience of young people. Almost immediately, the reader is told that the car has a 'powerful' 85 brake horsepower and a top speed of 109 mph. Again, this information would probably not be at the top of the agenda if Toyota was going for the middle-aged, supermarket audience. In addition, we are told that the Yaris has 'sports suspension, a rear-roof spoiler, 15" alloy wheels and ABS'. This information has clearly been selected with image-conscious buyers in mind. The price of the Yaris – £10,945, cheap for what Toyota are claiming is a 'performance' car – is placed in the main body of the advertisement rather than in the small print at the end. Putting this information in such a prominent position can only suggest that Toyota consider this a key selling point. The same must be true of the fact that its average fuel consumption is an impressive 47.1 mpg, another piece of information that is highlighted. The combination of power and economy is no doubt one that Toyota believe will be extremely attractive to a young audience who want credibility without having to pay too high a price for it.

Task 3

Key Features
Comments on advertisements should consider the medium they appear in, and the audience that medium caters for. They should also consider the likely kind of consumer of the product advertised.

1. Write down **four** pieces of evidence provided in the first paragraph that suggest the Toyota Yaris advert is targeted towards a **young audience**.

2. Choose an advert from a magazine. Explain who you believe the target audience is. You should consider the features in the left-hand column.

Target audience

	For example …
the type of product being sold	a pair of trainers
the magazine the advert comes from	Arena
the language of the advert	the streets
its visual appearance	a man running through a tough neighbourhood
the information it contains	the design of the trainers' soles

Before you begin, explain who you think the target audience is for the trainers in the example. List the five pieces of evidence in order of importance.

Task 4

Key Features
The information given in advertisements helps us understand their purpose.

1. List **eight** pieces of information provided to support the idea that the Yaris is being sold as a car that combines **power** with **economy**.

2. Leon O'Driscoll cannot be sure that what he is saying is true because he did not write the Yaris advert. He is **speculating**. Write down **five** words and phrases (in addition to the two below) that help O'Driscoll show the reader he is speculating. Your list should begin:

   - probably
   - suggests

3. On two occasions, O'Driscoll seems to be **certain** of what he is saying. Write down the two phrases he uses to show the reader this.

8 pieces of information

Media Coursework Task

Choose an advertisement from a magazine. Comment on how it is attempting to sell a product.

You will need to write about:

- **who** the advert is targeted towards (the audience)

- the **language** being used to sell the product

- the **information** the advertisers have chosen

- the way the **visual appearance** of the advert helps to sell the product

- the **magazine** the advert appears in.

EXAMINER'S TIP

To get a Grade 'C' you need to explain the *effects of language, presentational devices and visual images upon response.* So you must say why the language and appearance of the advert would appeal to a particular target audience.

To get a Grade 'A' you must *show analytical and interpretative skill* when you do the above. You can do this by going beyond obvious comments about how the advert is trying to reach its audience. The A* passage in *Other Students' Work* is an example of someone going into analytical depth about the way an advert's language and appearance is targeting women in middle age.

Other Students' Work

The following extracts represent achievement at GCSE Grades 'F', 'C' and 'A*'. They are taken from assignments written about an Elizabeth Arden skin product.

target audience

 F This advert was <u>written for women</u> because it has a woman in the picture who is smiling and she looks happy. She's really rich and happy because she uses Elizabeth Arden cream for her skin and it makes it look young and no wrinkles. The woman in the picture is <u>nice looking and she is laughing</u> and she can afford to spend a lot of money on skin cream.

visual appearance of advert

● has not said how key features influence response of target audience

visual appearance

 C This advert is almost certainly written for women because it is women that normally buy face cream. The woman in the advertisement looks <u>happy and contented</u> because she has just used the face cream and she is pleased with the way she looks. She is not very young – about 40 years old – and <u>she thinks the face cream has given back her youth</u>. The advert's headline is '<u>for all the laughter that lies ahead of me</u>'. It's like saying that, although she's old, the woman in the picture has still got a happy life in the future, not only in her memories of being young.

focus on language

effect of product

specific target audience

 A* The advert is targeted towards <u>women in middle age who are becoming insecure</u> about their looks. The central image of the advert is a happy-looking, 40-something, running her hand through her hair and smiling, as if at a private joke. The 'private joke', of course, is the secret information she has recently discovered: that using <u>Elizabeth Arden face cream makes you look, feel and behave like the young person you once were</u>. This absurd visual imagery is supported by the text. The header talks about the '<u>laughter that lies ahead of you</u>', a reference to the fact that not only is there a life ahead (despite your age) but that it will be a happy one (despite your skin) because Elizabeth Arden will sort your wrinkles out for you. The word '<u>ahead</u>' is bolded and capitalised to suggest the importance of looking to the future. <u>The language then goes on to mystify the product</u> in order to make it appear capable of the miracles it claims. Instead of referring to it as 'skin cream', the advertisers talk about 'Millenium Energist Revitalising Emulsion': with a name like that, who could fail to believe it worked? I'm not sure why they spell Millennium with one 'n' but <u>I think it may be to give it a French, sophisticated feel</u>.

message of advert

focus on language

detailed language focus

analytical skill

effect of language

Your Final Check-list

As you go through your various assignments keep a check-list of what you have done. This is one way of ensuring all the written pieces are present in your coursework folder, and that you have completed all the Speaking assignments required. More importantly, this will help you track the skills you have learned.

Have you?	YES	NO	GO TO UNIT
Covered the Reading components?			
● Explore			4
● Analyse			5
● Review			11
● Comment			12
Covered the Writing components?			
● Imagine			6
● Entertain			10
● Review			11
● Comment			12
Covered the Speaking/Listening components?			
● Explain			1
● Describe			2
● Narrate			3
● Imagine			6
● Discuss			7
● Argue			8
● Persuade			9
Can you?			
● Compare between and within texts			4 & 5
● Refer to stagecraft in plays			5
● Comment on social, cultural, historical features			4 & 5
● Use stereotypes and settings in narratives			10
● Recognise and use powerful language choices in narratives			6 & 10
● Conduct discussions in reflective, positive ways			4, 6, 7
● Use language choices consciously to influence and persuade			8, 9, 12
● Explain personal experiences clearly and informatively			1, 2, 3
● Present and explain opinions on non-fiction texts			11 & 12
Finally ...			
● Do you know what makes the difference between one grade and another?			1–12